Discover the
Southwestern Adirondacks

Four-Season Adventures in the
Wild-Forested Foothills

D0707339

Shingle Mill Falls

Discover the Southwestern Adirondacks

Four-Season Adventures in the Wild-Forested Foothills

Lee M. Brenning
William P. Ehling
Barbara McMartin

with the assistance of Stanford Pulrang

Backcountry Publications
Woodstock, Vermont

An Invitation to the Reader
Over time trails can be rerouted and signs and landmarks altered. If you find that changes have occurred on the routes described in this book, please let us know so that corrections may be made in future editions. The author and publisher also welcome other comments and suggestions. Address all correspondence to:

Editor
Discover the Adirondacks Series
Backcountry Publications
P.O. Box 175
Woodstock, VT 05091

Library of Congress Cataloging-in-Publication Data

McMartin, Barbara.
  Discover the southwestern Adirondacks.

  (Discover the Adirondacks series)
  Bibliography: p. 218
  Includes index.
    1. Hiking—New York (State)—Adirondack Mountains—
  Guide-books. 2. Outdoor recreation—New York (State)—
  Adirondack Mountains—Guide-books. 3. Adirondack
  Mountains (N.Y.)—Description and travel—Guide-books.
  I. Brenning, Lee M., 1955–   . II. Ehling, Bill,
  1920–   . III. Title. IV. Series.
  GV199.42.N652A3444 1987   917.47′53′043   87-994
  ISBN 0-942440-36-6 (pbk.)

Published by Backcountry Publications, Inc.
Woodstock, Vermont 05091
Printed in the United States of America by McNaughton & Gunn
Typesetting by The Sant Bani Press

Series design by Leslie Fry
Layout by Barbara McMartin
Maps by Richard Widhu

Photograph credits

Barbara McMartin, 2, 6, 11, 22, 25, 35, 36, 42, 44, 48, 50, 57, 85, 87, 89, 110, 112, 123, 127, 129, 132, 152, 181, 185, 187, 197, 200, 209.
Lee M. Brenning, 20, 54, 62, 66, 70, 75, 78, 91, 97, 118, 139, 142.
William P. Ehling, 12, 159, 166, 193, 200, 209, 214, 218-219.

Acknowledgements

While this guide was the joint effort of all three authors, each was in turn assisted by many others, to whom we are all indebted.

Barbara's husband, W. Alec Reid, helped all three authors by expertly printing all their black and white photographs. She was assisted also by Stanford Pulrang, who discovered and researched many parts of the Ferris Lake Wild Forest and planned and led excursions to explore that region. Willard (Bill) Reed researched two of the longest hikes in the southern area.

Lee Brenning's wife Georgie travelled with him on almost all the miles of trails and canoe routes that he researched. She added new perspective and sensitivity to their joint explorations as only a true "woodsie" can.

Ron Canter, who wrote on Little Black Creek, continues to discover some of the most unusual canoe routes in the Adirondacks.

James C. Dawson serves as geologist for the series and added notes on Panther Dam.

Our historical research took us to many sources. We would like to thank Dorothea Ives, the Kirby Free Library of Salisbury, the Oneida County Historical Society of Lyons Falls, John Norton, proprietor of the Otter Lake General Store, and Ted and Bruce Koenig, who run logging operations near North Lake.

In addition, all three authors were assisted by many DEC rangers and other personnel: Rangers John Seifts of Lake Pleasant, Doug Reidman of Old Forge, Steve Bazan of Ohio, Robert Henrickson of Brantingham, and Barb Keleher of the Nick Lake Campground Staff; Scott K. Gray III, Assistant Forester, Region 6, Lowville; and Elmer Erwin, Regional Forester, Region 6, Canton.

We want to thank all of them along with the numerous residents and camp owners who talked to us about the woods.

Train along an Esker near Evies Pond

Contents

BLACK RIVER WILD FOREST

Nelson Lake

Fish Creek

Introduction

THIS GUIDE COVERS an area that rings the southwestern Adirondacks, the low foothills that are easily reached from central Mohawk Valley cities. No single highway touches all of the area; no road system easily circles the region so you could become acquainted with it before trying its trails. There are no dramatic mountain tops, so the relatively little change in elevation will not attract the mountain climber. However, once you begin to explore the region, you will be impressed with the enormous variation in terrain and forest cover and the range of outdoor activities that cover all seasons.

The southwestern Adirondacks is a place for nature lovers, those who want to be close to wildlife, those who delight in a sphagnum bog or a pine-crowned sandy ridge. It is a place for those who like long, level trails or well-groomed routes for hiking. If you want to feel as if the whole forest is yours to enjoy in solitary quiet, this is the place for you. Weekend hikers will only occasionally meet others on the trail; those fortunate enough to walk in midweek will encounter only deer and birds and, rarely, signs of a bear. The walks are gentle, mirroring the gentle blue hills you see as you approach the region. Much of the forest floor is open, a contrast with the dense growth of the eastern Adirondacks.

Much of the region is visited only by hunters, fishermen, and snowmobilers. Dirt roads and blocks of private lands are scattered throughout the region, so the public land is classified Wild Forest by the State Land Master Plan. This means that a wide variety of recreation is possible, from backpacking to snowmobiling. Roads, man-made structures such as lean-tos and bridges, and motorized vehicles such as snowmobiles and all-terrain vehicles (ATVs) are allowed on parts of the state land. This is in contrast with areas to the east which are designated Wilderness, where no roads, few structures, and no vehicles are permitted.

The guide begins in the south with the western portion of the Ferris Lake Wild Forest. The entire Black River Wild Forest to the north is included. The Independence River Wild Forest on the western rim of the park is the most northerly area in this guide. Most of the old roads in the Independence River Wild Forest are snowmobile trails and quite a few can be used by all-terrain vehicles. There is road access to many streams and several lakes for those who do not hike. Old roads throughout the region make good hiking routes for those who wish a firm footing.

Southern portions receive deep snows, deeper than those in most of the rest of the Adirondacks. This combined with relatively level trails makes it a place for cross-country skiers. In recent years, the numbers of skiers in some areas have grown to equal those who use snowmobiles and the trend will continue.

ACCESS

Access to the region from the Mohawk Valley in the Utica area is along NY 8 and 12. NY 8 swings east to cross the area, separating the Ferris Lake Wild Forest on the south from the Black River Wild Forest in the north. NY 28 makes a longer loop to the north, bordering the northern reaches of the Black River Wild Forest. A number of roads penetrate the forest, and you should have a good map to assist in locating the trailheads.

How to Use the "Discover" Guides

The regional guides in this *Discover the Adirondacks* series will tell you enough about each area so that you can enjoy it any time of the year, in many different ways. Each guide will acquaint you with that region's access roads and trailheads, its trails and unmarked paths, some bushwhack routes and canoe trips, and its best picnic spots, campsites, and ski-touring routes. At the same time, the guides will introduce you to valleys, mountains, cliffs, scenic views, lakes, streams, and a myriad of other natural features.

Some of the destinations are within walking distance of the major highways that ring the areas, while others are miles deep into the wilderness. Each description will enable you to determine the best excursion for you and to enjoy the natural features you will pass, whether you are on a summer day hike or a winter ski-touring trek. The sections are grouped in chapters according to their access points; each chapter contains a brief introduction to that area's history and the old settlements and industries that have all but disappeared into wilderness. Throughout the guides you will find accounts of the geological forces that shaped features of the land. Unusual wildflowers and forest stands also will be pointed out.

It is our hope that you will find this guide not only an invitation to know and enjoy the woods but a companion for all your adventures there.

MAPS AND NOMENCLATURE

The Adirondack Atlas, a map published by City Street Directory of Poughkeepsie, New York, is the best reference for town roads, and it has the added advantage of identifying state land. In spite of the fact that it has not been updated to show recent acquisitions, this is a valuable help in the southwestern region where public and private lands are so intricately mixed.

This guide contains maps that show all the routes mentioned, but you may still want to carry the USGS for the region. Unfortunately, part of the region is covered by the 15-minute series and part by the 7.5-minute series. This not only complicates following some routes, but it means you might need quite a few maps. The maps in this guide are adequate to cover the areas for which the USGS has only 7.5-minute maps, but you may want Stratford, Salisbury, Hinckley, North Wilmurt, Port Leyden, Brantingham, and Crystal Dale, depending on the areas that interest you. You will want the 15 minute maps for Ohio, McKeever, Piseco, and Number Four. While most sporting goods stores carry the 15-minute series, the 7.5-minute series are not as generally available locally. For these you may have to write the USGS Map Distribution Branch, Box 25286, Denver Federal Center, Denver, CO 80225. Maps from the USGS are currently $2.50 each. At this time, maps are more easily obtained from a private source, Timely Discount Maps. You can call them with their phone number 1-800-821-7609. They will usually ship maps in 10 days with an invoice.

The guide uses the spelling given in the USGS but local variations are noted.

DISTANCE AND TIME

Distance along the routes is measured from the USGS survey maps and is accurate to within ten percent. Few hikers gauge distance accurately even on well-defined trails. Distance is a variable factor in comparing routes along trails, paths, or bushwhacks.

Time is given as an additional gauge for the length of routes. It gives a better understanding of the difficulty of the terrain, the change of elevation, and the problems of finding a suitable course. Average time for walking trails is 2 miles an hour, 3 miles if the way is level and well defined; for paths, 1½ to 2 miles an hour; and for bushwhacks, 1 mile an hour.

Summaries for distance, time, and vertical rise are given with the title of each section describing a trail or path. These distances and times are for *one way only*, unless otherwise stated.

TYPES OF ROUTES

Each section of this guide generally describes a route or a place. Included in the descriptions are such basic information as the suitability for different levels of woods experience, walking (or skiing, paddling, and climbing) times, distances, directions to the access, and, of course, directions along the route itself. The following definitions clarify the terms used in this book.

A route is considered a *trail* if it is so designated by the New York State Department of Environmental Conservation (DEC). This means the trail is routinely cleared by DEC or volunteer groups and adequately marked with official DEC disks. *Blue disks* generally indicate major north-south routes, *red disks* indicate east-west routes, and *yellow disks* indicate side trails. This scheme is not, however, applied consistently throughout the Adirondacks.

Some trails have been marked for *cross-country skiing,* and new *pale yellow disks with a skier* are used. *Large orange disks* indicate *snowmobile trails,* which are limited to some portions of Wild Forest Areas. Snowmobiles are permitted on them in winter when there is sufficient snow cover. Many snowmobile trails on the interior are not heavily used and can be shared by those on cross-country skis as long as the skier is cautious. Hikers can enjoy both ski and snowmobile trails.

A *path* is an informal and unmarked route with a clearly defined foot tread. These traditional routes, worn by fishermen and hunters to favorite spots, are great for hiking. A path, however, is not necessarily kept open, and fallen trees and new growth sometimes obliterate its course. The paths that cross wet meadows or open fields often become concealed by lush growth. You should always carry a map and compass when you are following an unmarked path and you should keep track of your location.

There is a safe prescription for walking paths. In a group of three or more hikers, stringing out along a narrow path will permit the leader to scout until the path disappears, at which point at least one member of the party should still be standing on an obvious part of the path. If that hiker remains standing while those in front range out to find the path, the whole group can continue safely after a matter of moments.

Hikers in the north country often use the term *bushwhack* to describe an uncharted and unmarked trip. Sometimes bushwhacking means literally pushing brush aside, but it usually connotes a variety of cross-country walks.

Bushwhacks are an important part of this regional guide series because of the shortage of marked trails throughout much of the Adirondack Park and the abundance of little-known and highly desirable destinations for which no visible routes exist. While experienced bushwhackers could reach these destinations with not much more help than the knowledge of their location, I think most hikers will appreciate these simple descriptions that point out the easiest and most interesting routes and the possible pitfalls. In general, descriptions for bushwhacks are less detailed than those for paths or trails, for the guide assumes that those who bushwhack have a greater knowledge of the woods than those who walk marked routes.

I have defined a *bushwhack* as any trip on which you make your way through the woods without a trail, path, or the visible foot tread of other hikers and without markings, signs, or blazes. It also means you will make your way by following a route chosen on a contour map, aided by a compass, using streambeds, valleys, abandoned roads, and obvious ridges as guides. Most bushwhacks require navigating by both contour map and compass and an understanding of the terrain.

Bushwhack distances are not given in precise tenths of a mile. They are estimates representing the shortest distance you could travel between points. This reinforces the fact that each hiker's cross-country route will be different, yielding different mileages.

A bushwhack is said to be *easy* if the route is along a stream, a lakeshore, a reasonably obvious abandoned roadway, or a similar well-defined feature. A short route to the summit of a hill or a small mountain can often be easy. A bushwhack is termed *moderate* if a simple route can be defined on a contour map and followed with the aid of a compass. Previous experience is necessary. A bushwhack is rated *difficult* if it entails a complex route, necessitating advanced knowledge of navigation by compass and reading contour maps and land features.

Compass directions for bushwhacks are given in degrees from magnetic north, a phrase abbreviated here to *degrees magnetic*.

The guide occasionally refers to old *blazed* lines or trails. The word "blaze" comes from the French *blesser* and means to cut or wound. Early loggers and settlers made deep slashes in good-sized trees with an ax to mark property lines and trails. Later, hunters and fishermen often made slashes with knives and, though they are not as deep as ax cuts, they too can still be seen. Following an old blazed path for miles in dense woods is often a challenging but good way to reach a trailless destination. Remember, though, that it is now, and has been for many years, illegal to deface trees in the Forest Preserve in this manner.

You may see *yellow paint daubs on a line of trees*. These lines usually indicate the boundary between private and public lands. Individuals have also used different colors of paint to mark informal routes from time to time. Although it is not legal to mark trails on state land, this guide does refer to such informally marked paths.

All *vehicular traffic*, except snowmobiles on their designated trails, is *prohibited* in the Forest Preserve. There are some town roads or roads that lead to private inholdings on which vehicular use is permitted. These roads are described in the guides, and soon the DEC will start marking those old roads that are open to vehicles. Most old roads referred to in the guides are town or logging roads that were abandoned when the land around them became part of the Forest Preserve. Now they are routes for hikers, not for vehicles.

There has been an increase in the use of three- and four-wheeled off-road vehicles, even on trails where such use is not permitted. New laws will stop this use in the Forest Preserve and make sure that some of the old roads remain attractive hiking routes.

Cables have been placed across many streams by hunters and other sportsmen to help them cross in high water. The legality of this practice has been questioned. Some may be quite safe to use, others are certainly questionable. Using them is not a recommended practice, so when this guide mentions crossing streams to reach some of the hikes, you are urged to do so only when a boat can be used or in low water when you can walk across.

The *beginning of each section describing a trail* gives a summary of the distance, time, and elevation change for the trail. For unmarked routes, such information is given only within the text of each section, partly to allow for the great variations in the way hikers approach an unmarked route and partly to emphasize the difficulty of those routes.

Protecting the Land

Most of the land described in these guides is in the *Forest Preserve*, land set aside a century ago, where no trees may be cut. All of it is open to the public. The *Adirondack Park Agency* has responsibility for the Wilderness, Primitive, and Wild Forest guidelines that govern use of the Forest Preserve. Care and custody of these state lands is left to the Department of Environmental Conservation, which is in the process of producing Unit Management Plans for the roughly 130 separate Forest Preserve areas.

Camping is permitted throughout the public lands except at elevations above 4000 feet and within 150 feet of water or 100 feet of trails. In certain fragile areas, camping is restricted to specific locations, and the state is using a new No Camping disk to mark fragile spots. *Permits* for camping on state lands are needed only for stays that exceed three days or for groups of more than ten campers. Permits can be obtained from the local rangers, who are listed in the area phone books under NY DEC.

Only dead and downed wood can be used for *campfires*. Build fires only when absolutely necessary; carry a small stove for cooking. Build fires at designated fire rings or on rocks or gravelly soil. Fire is dangerous and can travel rapidly through the duff or organic soil, burning roots and spreading through the forest. Douse fires with water, and be sure they are completely out and cold before you leave.

Private lands are generally not open to the public, though some individuals have granted public access across their land to state land. It is always wise to ask before crossing private lands. Be very respectful of private landowners so that public access will continue to be granted. Never enter private lands that have been posted unless you have the owner's permission. Unless the text expressly identifies an area as state-owned Forest Preserve or private land whose owner permits unrestricted public passage, the inclusion of a walk description in this guide does not imply a public right-of-way.

Burn combustible trash and carry out everything else.

Most *wildflowers and ferns* mentioned in the text are protected by law. Do not pick them or try to transplant them.

Safety in the Woods

It is best *not to walk alone.* Make sure someone knows where you are heading and when you are expected back.

Carry water or other liquids with you. Not only are the mountains dry, but the recent spread of *Giardia* makes many streams suspect. I have an aluminum fuel bottle especially for carrying water; it is virtually indestructible and has a deep screw that prevents leaking.

Carry a small *day pack* with insect repellent, flashlight, first aid kit, emergency food rations, waterproof matches, jackknife, whistle, rain gear, and a wool sweater, even for summer hiking. Wear layers of wool and waterproof clothing in winter and carry an extra sweater and socks. If you plan to camp, consult a good outfitter or a camping organization for the essentials. Better yet, make your first few trips with an experienced leader or with a group.

Always carry a *map and compass.* You may also want to carry an altimeter to judge your progress on the bushwhack climbs.

Wear *glasses* when bushwhacking. The risk to your eyes of a small protruding branch makes this a necessity.

Do carry *binoculars* for birding as well as for viewing distant peaks.

Use great care near the *edges of cliffs* and when *crossing streams* by hopping rocks in the streambed. Never bushwhack unless you have gained a measure of woods experience. If you are a novice in the out-of-doors, join a hiking group or hire the services of one of the many outfitters in the north country. As you get to know the land, you can progress from the standard trails to the more difficult and more satisfyingly remote routes. Then you will really begin to discover the Adirondacks.

Beaver Marsh near Nicks Creek

Western Ferris Lake Wild Forest

THE FERRIS LAKE Wild Forest is an immense tract in the southern Adirondacks; only its western region is included in this guide. It is a place of many lakes, rolling hills, numerous inholdings, and maturing second-growth forests. Many small streams flow southwest to join Black Creek, whose watershed comprises most of this chapter.

There are no trails designed expressly for the hiker, but with a little work, you can visit many inviting destinations. The best season of all for the region is the winter, for this is an area of deep snows. The vlies that punctuate the dense forest can best be enjoyed when they are frozen. The attractiveness and accessibility of the region means that snowshoeing and cross-country skiing will continue to increase in popularity. Here is a region for the adventurous to explore and revel in a sense of discovery.

Black Creek

The Southwestern Corner of the Park

THE SOUTHWESTERN CORNER of the Adirondack Park touches farming communities in townships with such intriguing names as Poland, Russia, and Norway. The area just outside the Park, accessible from state highways 29, 8, and 28, contains rich dairy lands, famous since the mid-nineteenth century for cheese. As you drive northeast into the Park from the valley of the West Canada Creek, either along NY 8 northeast from Poland or NY 29 east from Middleville, you climb steadily onto the western Adirondack plateau. Numerous small roads lead to abandoned farms and recovering forests, but the area is peppered with second homes and private land so there are few state trails, and most of them are old roads marked for snowmobiles.

You can start discovering the southwestern Adirondacks along one of two routes, one a canoe trip, the other a very short walk. Either of them is a pleasant introduction to the region.

1 Black Creek
Canoe trip
13.1 miles, 5 hours

Black Creek rises in a cluster of ponds that lie near the eastern boundary of this guide, deep in Forest Preserve lands. After flowing west to Black Creek Reservoir on the boundary of the Park, Black Creek heads northwest to Hinckley Reservoir. This portion is entirely surrounded by private lands. In fact, the only public land in the southwestern corner of the Park is the state campground on Hinckley Reservoir north of the hamlet of Grant, which you may want to use as a base in the area or for boating on the reservoir.

The water of Black Creek is flat and canoeable for 10.6 miles upstream from Grant. That distance is just over 6 miles as the crow flies, but the river's meanders and oxbows add the difference. Don't be put off by the fact that its shores are private land. You will pass four bridges and see as

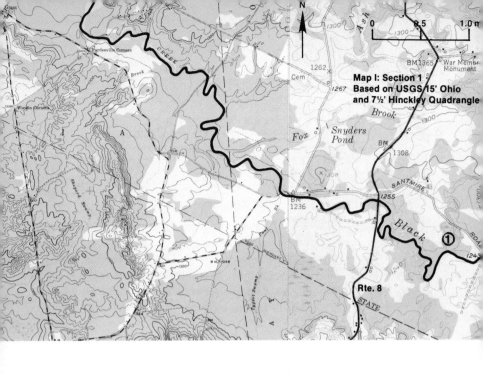

many houses, but all of the rest of the trip is as wild and secluded as you could wish. Given its accessibility and variety of birds and trees, it has to be a favorite. Five hours will suffice for the trip outlined, which includes paddling both up and downstream on the upper reaches.

The stream is canoeable even in low summer water, though then you may have to pull your canoe over an occasional shallow stretch. In spring or in high-water times, the stream is still flat, with a current that is rarely above 0.5 mile per hour.

To spot a car at Grant, drive east on NY 8 from Poland to Cold Brook and follow the signs north to Grant, a total of 5.5 miles from the West Canada Valley. There is a hotel on the northwest side of the bridge. Ask there to leave your car in the parking area.

Drive back across the bridge. Take the first left, Pardeeville Road, and drive 2.5 miles to a left turn on Fisher Road. In 1.4 miles you make a left turn and continue 1.2 miles to NY 8. There is a large gravel parking area on the east side of NY 8. Slide your canoe down the steep bank to the stream.

As an alternative, you can shorten the trip by 2.5 miles by driving east from the parking area on Santmire Road for 1.4 miles to a dirt track which leads south 100 yards to an old iron bridge over Black Creek. This, too, is a steep place to launch. Study the river downstream from the bridge to be sure there is enough water to launch here.

From NY 8 it is 2.5 miles by canoe upstream to the bridge, and the stream is pretty enough to justify paddling both ways. It starts out in a long meander paralleling NY 8, but as soon as it turns away, you are in a world of wetland wonder. Tall elms grow beside the creek amidst willow, hawthorn, cherry, and American hornbeam. Families of ducks will scoot ahead of your canoe. Warblers perch on overhanging branches. You may see yellow or black and white warblers and you will hear many more. Cedar waxwings, kingfishers, kingbirds, and flycatchers abound in the snags that dot the wetlands along both sides of the creek. Joe-Pye weed, Canada lilies, and virgin's bower grace the shore.

Marked layers define the steep, muddy banks around each curve in the creek, whose entire length is carved through mud and sand flats. You see very few rocks until you reach the two long, straight stretches that end at the iron bridge. In those stretches, you will find shores darkened with spruce, a sight more typical of northern streams.

It will take about an hour and ten minutes to paddle upstream to the iron bridge; fifty minutes will suffice for a leisurely return.

The 1.3-mile stretch of river east to the next bridge is a transition from the upriver wetlands, for tall popple and hemlock and pine begin to appear. Beyond the bridge, steep sand banks covered with pine and hemlock border the creek. The creek narrows and is overhung with birches and

Wildlife on Black Creek

hemlock. Blue flag, elderberry, hellebore, and many ferns appear in small patches beneath the hawthorns. After a twisting 2.5 miles, you reach the crumbling abutment of an abandoned bridge.

Shoreline cover opens up in the next 1.9 miles to the bridge over Pardeeville Road. In the last 2.4-mile segment before Grant, the creek is very wide, with more loops than ever. It is bordered with marshes that are home to many heron and ducks. You finish the trip at Grant at the edge of a bay that opens into the Reservoir.

There are no dry places to stop for a picnic, so plan to drift while eating and birding.

2 Dairy Hill

Birding, fire tower, views into the Forest Preserve

No mileages are given for this tower visit, which lies just outside the Forest Preserve northwest of Salisbury Center, because you can actually drive to the tower. However, the dirt road leading to the tower is a delightful bird walk.

With a good map you can find the tower by driving east from Newport on NY 28. An alternate route heads east on NY 29 from Middleville, up the hill past the beautiful stone arch of the earlier road, through Fairfield, once home to an early academy, and on up the escarpment to the crest with its panoramic view of the West Canada Valley and the fringes of the Mohawk Valley. NY 29 takes you to the corner in Salisbury where you turn left, north, on the Military Road. Continue straight on the paved road, which is County Road 36. Old maples line the roadway, which turns left 7 miles from Salisbury.

As you approach the crest of the hill, pause beside the road. You have almost the same view as from the tower, north to the gentle foothills of the Adirondacks, but here across fields where bobolinks nest. Just beyond the crest of the hill, turn left on Observatory Road, a dirt road that heads south to a left fork for the tower. If you walk the dirt road you are sure to find birds in the marsh that borders it, part way to the tower. Then as you make the turn to the tower, look carefully in the sheltering trees. Indigo buntings nest here.

The tower is manned and the observer will help you identify the distant hills that border NY 8 and reach into the Canada Lake Wilderness Area. The rest of the walks described in this chapter lie nestled in the nearby hills.

Bull Hill Trails

BULL HILL ROAD leads to several trails. You can reach it from Gray, a crossroads east of NY 8. Take the east road at the crossroads for 0.6 mile to reach Bull Hill Road. From the south and east, take Black Creek Road, a north fork from County Route 36, section 2. Black Creek Road passes the dam on Black Creek Reservoir that served the City of Utica. Where the road crosses the creek, a historic marker tells that a raiding force of Tories, led by Major Ross and Walter Butler, was here attacked by Col. Marinus Willett's patriot soldiers on October 30, 1781. Just north of the marker, turn right, east, on Bull Hill Road.

3 Mounts Creek Trail

Snowmobile trail
5.5 miles, 2 hours, relatively level

Bull Hill Road turns to the north and becomes Billy Hamlin Road after it passes Coonradt Road. After 0.9 mile, Billy Hamlin Road turns right, due east. The old road that heads straight north at this point is marked as a snowmobile trail with a guideboard stating 2.2 miles to Mounts Creek Lake, 14.5 miles to Morehouseville, and 23 miles to Piseco. Unless much trailwork has been done, that sign is optimistic, for the middle section of this route is full of blowdowns and overgrown with witch hobble. In addition, it just seems to disappear in a grassy vly.

You can follow the trail north for about 5 miles. The hiking is not very exciting; and, for some people, there are barely enough hills to make good cross-country skiing. The northern end of the trail, section 21, is much more interesting. However, if trailwork is done—and none is currently anticipated—this will make an excellent through ski trip of 12.5 miles. The fact that the trail no longer extends to Morehouseville is not the only misleading information on the sign; Mounts Creek Lake is nearly 4 miles away and not on the trail at all.

Mounts Creek derives its name from a family of settlers who tried to farm near where the Creek crosses the Gray Wilmurt Road in the 1700s. While the parents sought supplies in the Mohawk Valley, Indians raided the farm, scalping two sons. A daughter survived by hiding in a Dutch oven.

The trail starts on private land where vehicles are used to reach a private inholding. It heads northeast and begins by descending to cross the

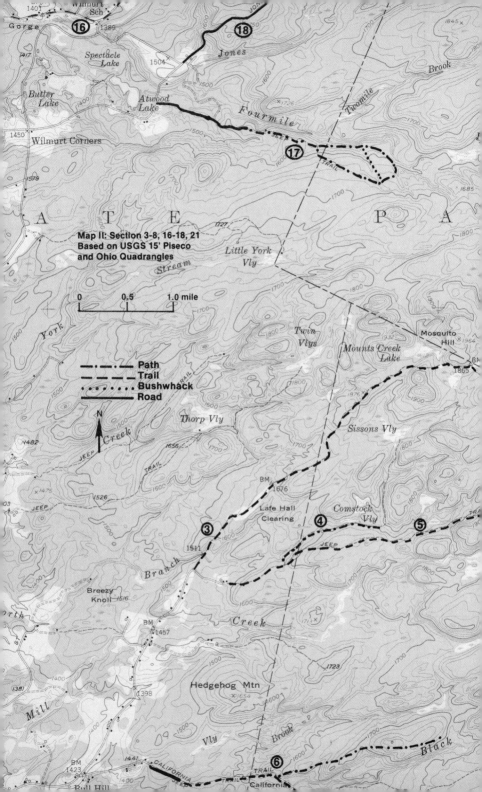

Map II: Section 3-8, 16-18, 21
Based on USGS 15' Piseco
and Ohio Quadrangles

0   0.5   1.0 mile

— · — · — Path
— — — — Trail
· · · · · · Bushwhack
———— Road

N

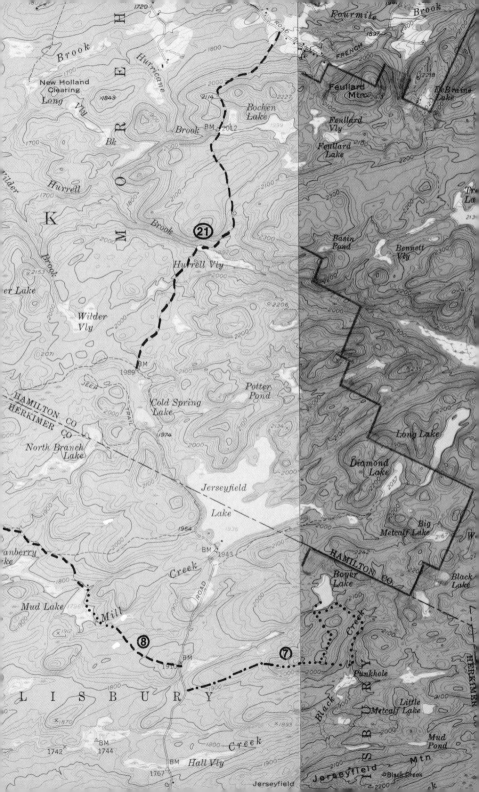

North Branch of Black Creek at 0.2 mile. After a gentle climb, the roadway levels out to pass a large clearing and some marshy areas. At 1.2 miles you will see posted signs and a field on the right. This is Lafe Hall Clearing. Here the trail forks with the way left leading to a camp. A sign points to French Road (in Morehouseville) on the right fork, which now has snowmobile trail markers.

The trail, still heading generally northeast, is not nearly as open as at the beginning, though the ruts from vehicles persist. At 1.6 miles you reach state land, clearly marked with warnings that no motorized vehicles except snowmobiles are permitted. In the next mile the trail crosses an intermittent stream and takes a northerly direction. If you look carefully, you will notice a path marked with red tin cans forking left, west. This leads to a grassy vly.

Returning to a northeasterly direction, the trail climbs slightly, dips, and reaches a height-of-land at about 3 miles. In the descent that follows, blowdowns begin to fill the trail. The point where the trail takes an easterly direction, at about 3.6 miles, is the closest approach to Mounts Creek Lake, which lies hidden nearly 0.2 mile north of the trail. A small hill follows, then, at about 4 miles you see swampy areas off to your right. The trail briefly takes on a southeasterly direction and the blowdowns increase. The next thing you know you are in the middle of a swamp. You cross a small stream that flows to your left, northwest, toward Mounts Creek Lake, but dense alders surround the stream.

Beyond the swamp, the trail hugs the south side of a small hill, a shoulder of Mosquito Hill—that name aptly describes the flat region to the east through which the old roadway used to pass. There is a large swampy area to the south at this point. If you cross the small stream that is the outlet of Deer Lake on a beaver dam, you can continue east on the trail for a short distance more. In a clearing with an old apple tree and signs of past logging or a settlement, the trail seems to disappear. It can be followed east for a bit further, but without trailwork this is effectively the end of the road. Even if the trail were easier to find, blowdowns make skiing further very difficult.

4 Comstock Vly

Part snowmobile trail, skiing
4.5-mile loop, 2½ hours, relatively level

You can make a good ski trip out of this route, part of which follows an old road now used as a snowmobile trail, and part a path informally cleared along a second old road. In summer, use the route if you like to explore grassy vlies, though you may find it disturbing that jeeps and ATVs also use the route.

Drive north on Billy Hamlin Road to the right turn, section 3, and drive east for 0.4 mile. Park before the houses and do not block the continuing roadway. Take the jeep trail east for 0.7 mile, less than a fifteen-minute walk, to a nearly concealed fork to the left. The jeep trail has deep mud wallows—here defined as places four-wheel-drive vehicles go to luxuriate—and the fork is past the third wallow. That information will be of little help in winter. There are no really good features to help identify the turn, except to note that just east of it, after you pass it, the trail climbs a small hill. The continuing route is described in section 5.

You take the left fork, which is blazed. It heads just east of north, then swings to the east along the ridge line above the North Branch of Black Creek. At 0.7 mile the path comes within 100 yards of the creek. In the next 0.6 mile there are several points where you can glimpse the vly that surrounds the creek. After a thirty-minute walk from the fork, you reach a ford crossing at the head of Comstock Vly, which stretches both west and north. There is also a cable crossing just upstream and an improvised bridge.

Maps indicate that the old road turned north here and continued to Sissons Vly. No one has kept that route open and no sign of it can be found. You will enjoy skiing through and exploring the vlies—large grassy meadows surrounded by deep evergreen woods. The main snowmobile trail is quite close to the creek just east of the vly and you can easily bushwhack south to it for a return loop. Note that wet, undrained roadway makes horrible walking.

5 Cranberry Lake from the West

Snowmobile trail, skiing
4 miles, 1½ hours, 300-foot vertical rise

A marked snowmobile trail leads to watershed property on Mill Creek. The property is not posted and several groups have hunting cabins on the ponds along the creek. This trail used to run due east to intersect the private road on the west side of Jerseyfield Lake. With the posting of that property, the trail's eastern end was changed. See section 8.

This is not a good walking route because of the extensive vehicular use along it. The first part, described in section 4, is deeply rutted and wet. East of the fork, the road climbs nearly 100 feet but the ruts continue to make walking difficult for much of the first 2 miles. In the next mile, the trail is close enough to the North Branch of Black Creek that you can see it occasionally. Just short of 3 miles, the road climbs a hill and at 3.5 miles reaches an obvious fork. The way ahead leads to Mud Lake, section 8, and the way right leads south in 0.5 mile downhill, a drop of 100 feet, to Cranberry Lake.

Cranberry Lake was a dammed up portion of Mill Creek. The dam is out and the lovely grassy vly with stumps and boulders is a handsome place, with few visitors except in hunting season, perhaps attractive enough to justify the long, unappealing walk to reach it. In winter, with snow covering the problems of the road, the opportunity to ski around the mile-long flow makes this a most desirable destination.

6 California Clearing
Old roads, skiing

Call this an invitation to explore with promises unfulfilled. It is easy to understand the early settlers naming new settlements after places they had left, like Norway or Poland, but why California Clearing? In any event, the name may be more romantic than anything you will discover along this route. California Clearing, a delightful spot along Black Creek, is posted. The old road that led east from the clearing is now overgrown. The spot was once a small settlement with sawmill, school, and several homes.

Drive east on Bull Hill Road for 1 mile and notice the historical marker on the left denoting the 1824 settlement. The California Trail forks right 0.5 mile further. You can drive for a short distance; there is room to park along the road at 0.7 mile. Because of the camps and inholdings along the route, there is substantial vehicular use of the trail. The road crosses Vly Brook 1 mile from Bull Hill Road and continues generally east with several logging roads forking from the main route. At 2.4 miles, a walk of forty minutes, the road forks. The way right leads in 200 yards downhill to Black Creek and California Clearing. The way left leads to several camps and unexplored roadways. The main route now is just east of north along high ground above Black Creek and can be followed east to vlies along that creek.

Do this as a winter ski trip and see what you can discover. The distance traveled will be in proportion to the clearing done by those who hunt in these woods. At this time, the main route east, not shown on the USGS, is relatively clear, though not very exciting.

Jerseyfield Road

JERSEYFIELD LAKE IS the center of a large private inholding, one of the choice spots in the region. The lake itself is the largest in the region and the tract contains several small and very attractive ponds. It is entirely posted. The dirt road leading to the Jerseyfield property winds north from the intersection known as Curtis. That intersection can be reached from Salisbury and NY 29 by taking the first right fork on Military Road, which is called Curtis Road, or by taking House Hill Road and the eastern portion of Curtis Road north from Salisbury Center near the intersection of NY 29 and 29A. Jerseyfield Road heads north from the four-way intersection known as Curtis. All mileages along the road are given from this point.

Several old roads and a railroad cross Jerseyfield Road. Parts of their routes are described in the text, and others are just mentioned to inspire the adventurous.

The railroad owes its existence to a line built before 1913 for an iron mine in Irondale, see section 12. With no waterways and no highways to speed logs to market, extending the railroad was the least expensive way to reach the rich forests to the north, so a railroad was extended from Salisbury north through a small crossroads known as Curtis. It headed northeast toward Trammel Creek, then northwest toward the present Jerseyfield Road. The railroad crossed the road 7.5 miles north of Curtis near the site of a main camp for the railroad and logging operation.

Branches of the railroad headed west from here as well as northeast along the upper reaches of Trammel and Black creeks. Only traces of these portions can be found, but further south where the route has been cleared for local snowmobile trails, old ties mark the way and occasional iron tracks and spikes can be seen. Needless to say, the railroad and logging roads make inviting routes for the hiker and cross-country skier.

Two other bushwhacks can be made by following old roads that intersect the Jerseyfield Road; these are not detailed in the guide, but you may want to explore them. At 6.25 miles north, a faint track heads west to Crosby Vly.

A second route, a fairly well-defined path, leads east at the 7.3-mile mark. It is not described in detail because it lacks a definable destination, but it can be used to explore the northern reaches of Trammel Creek and the ridge that is Jerseyfield Mountain.

Note that in the winter time, Jerseyfield Road is plowed only as far north as Weaver Hill, 5.7 miles from Curtis. The road is barred at the Jerseyfield Preserve at 9.3 miles. You can ski the northern portions of the Jerseyfield Road up to the barrier and thus connect with some of the northern routes mentioned, but remember to account for this additional mileage when making winter plans.

7 Boyer Lake and the Punkhole
Bushwhack

This loop follows old roads and trails for the most part, but it is so long since they have been used or marked that you had better rely on bushwhacking skills. To make this a really good walk, a short bushwhack is added, making the trip a loop.

At 8.5 miles north of Curtis on the Jerseyfield Road, there is what looks like the beginning of a road to the right, with a cable across it. The path following this roadway north of east along a high ridge is distinct for about a mile. The forest was heavily logged before it was sold to the state, and the first mile is full of small beech and maple starts.

After a mile, the path climbs a small knob, with low land lying off to the north. Here the route becomes very indistinct, though there are old blazes on the trees made more than fifteen years ago. The route is east, then southeast, up the hillside to the top of the ridge, then it veers back to the northeast. If you are a good tracker, you will still be following the old roadway here. Look for a large erratic off to the south of the route.

From here on, the way to Boyer Lake is all bushwhack, though you will still find signs of the blazed route. After walking over a series of small knolls for fifteen minutes, you may see a red-marked path heading southeast. You will complete the loop along it, and do not be surprised if you do not spot it on the way out.

Continue on high ground, contouring, and heading generally north of east. At about 2 miles from the start, you find you are descending into a short valley. At this point, change your direction to north. You descend through a natural draw, which leads you in 0.2 mile to Boyer Lake near its outlet. If you miss to the west, you can follow this distant tributary of Black Creek upstream to the lake. You are unlikely to miss to the east, since that would involve climbing a distinct knob before descending to the lake.

Boyer Lake

Black Creek near Punkhole

Cross the outlet and walk along the north shore to a rocky point thrust into the lake. Here is a lovely camping and picnic spot, and it is obvious that fishermen do come to this place.

To continue, walk along the south shore to the southeast corner of the lake. There is a very obvious draw that descends from two knobs lying to the southeast. Bushwhack up the draw, a rise of less than 100 feet, then strike out in a southerly direction from the top of the draw. This 0.7-mile bushwhack will take little more than half an hour and will lead to Black Creek, which drains Black Creek Lake. The lake lies to the east on a plateau between here and the Powley-Piseco Road. The avid bushwhacker should note that you can make a through trip to the district of small lakes and ponds on the plateau and on east via the Brayhouse Gore, described in *Discover the (Southern) Adirondacks II.*

Black Creek is a gem of a creek, here flowing south, sometimes rock-strewn, sometimes filled with beaver marshes. As you head downstream along it, watch carefully. Within 200 yards, you should spot the bed of a northern spur of the old logging railroad. It is indistinct at first, and crosses to the east bank shortly after you pick it up. It follows the stream closely all the way to the Punkhole, a distance of about 0.5 mile. The Punkhole is a large meadow on the creek, the former site of a logging camp. Near the north end of the marsh, you will find the remains of a handsome old iron stove, and other artifacts, perhaps bits from a garbage dump, lie nearby.

This spot is in a sort of an island in the creek and if you head west from it, you will see the beginning of an old road that once led to it. This route is marked with old blazes and there is something of a foot tread to guide you along. The path climbs steeply a little north of west to intersect the road you began this trek on. When you reach the main trail, head west, but keep a sharp eye on the route. It is every bit as hard to follow along the top of the ridge going west as it was going east, maybe harder. Even with the series of little knobs, there are no real guideposts.

The route outlined covers nearly 6 miles and takes a minimum of four hours. An alternate route can be devised by attempting to follow the railroad bed west-southwest back to the Jerseyfield Road, 7.15 miles north of Curtis.

8 Mud and Cranberry Lakes
Path, hiking, snowshoeing, fishing

This route will take you past very attractive marshes and lakes and connects with the snowmobile trail from the west, section 5. However, a few parts of the way are soggy, so either make the trip in winter on snowshoes, or make sure you have high, waterproof boots.

At the top of a rise, 0.3 mile before the Jerseyfield Preserve, is a trailhead sign on the left reading "Trail to Bull Hill Road." This DEC snowmobile trail was originally marked to replace the portion of the traditional route west from Jerseyfield Lake. Local snowmobile groups have kept it open.

The trail heads northwest through the woods, gradually descending a hill that slopes to the north. After less than fifteen minutes of travel, you will cross an intermittent stream. Here the trail veers to the north, directly down the hillside. After a 0.8-mile walk, you come out of the woods into a partially flooded marsh on Mill Creek, which is the outlet of Jerseyfield Lake. No further trail markings are visible at this point. Directly in front of you, north across a few hundred yards of marsh, you can see where the snowmobile trail reenters the woods to ascend a hillside. This is supposed to be the official trail, rejoining the old Jerseyfield-Bull Hill Road, skirting both the posted lands of the Jerseyfield Preserve and other private but unposted land down Mill Creek to the west. It is neither used nor maintained and is virtually impossible to follow through blowdowns. Even most of the snowmobile markers are gone.

In winter, crossing Mill Creek is a simple matter if it is sufficiently frozen. Then you can bushwhack west to the continuing path sportsmen use in place of the official route. In summer, you can not cross the creek here. It is better to bushwhack west along the soggy south side of the flow for 0.3 mile. There is a path of sorts here that leads to the south side of Mill Creek, about 100 yards west of an old dam. The creek can be crossed either here or 200 feet downstream, where there is an old improvised footbridge, which from a distance looks just like a tree fallen across the stream. There is no proper path to the bridge. After crossing it with care, you can find a path that leads in 200 yards to a hunter's camp made of poles, chicken wire, and black plastic.

From this camp on there is a well-marked and easy-to-follow route, which winds north-northwest toward the north shore of Mud Lake. The route is marked with red ties and it leads in about 0.6 mile to the track from Bull Hill Road. You get a glimpse of Mud Lake after only a few minutes on this path. Shortly after it merges with the old roadway, you will see a cabin. Tacked to the cabin is a sign that says that it is a one-and-a-half-hour walk to Bull Hill. But in this day of ATVs, no one seems to make this 5-mile walk from the west along the roadway described in section 5.

If you return to the fork and continue west, you quickly reach an intersection, where a south fork heads toward Mill Creek and the north branch soon veers to the northwest for 0.2 mile. Here the route is again marked as a snowmobile trail. This is actually an intersection, though you may not recognize it as such. The way east, the new bypass, is here blocked with an old oil can and the way is as indistinguishable as the eastern end.

Follow the roadway northwest, crossing an inlet of Cranberry Lake and climbing up a small hill. You reach the intersection with the trail south to the lake, section 5, 1.5 miles from the cabin.

9 The Abandoned Railroad near Trammel Creek
Bushwhack and path

The railroad that was pushed north from Salisbury to haul out logs from the Jerseyfield area has been used in recent years as a local snowmobile trail. The southern portions are accessible only over private lands, but parts of it in the north make good routes for exploring.

The most northerly section comes close to the Jerseyfield Road 6.1 miles north of Curtis. Here there is a big bend and a hollow in the road. East of this point, beaver have dammed a small tributary of Black Creek just east of the road. The flow to the east, which is not shown on the current USGS, is quite pretty, but walking along the hillside on its south side is not easy. However, if you persevere for 0.5 mile, you will run into the railroad grade. The railroad crossed the marsh area and intersected the Jerseyfield Road a mile to the north. The northern portion has not been cleared in recent years, but the way south is easy to follow. The railroad stays to high ground, heading south of east from the marsh. In 0.5 mile you are above Trammel Creek at the railroad's closest (0.2 mile) approach to it. It will take about ten minutes to bushwhack downhill 100 feet to the creek, and that is well worth doing for you can follow the creek south past two lovely marshy areas.

The railroad continues on a southerly course, between two hills, then swings east around them and continues a sinuous route following a relatively level grade on the hillside above the creek. After making a switchback above one of the creek's tributaries, the railroad bed changes direction to southwest for 2.5 miles, then continues south for just over 2.5 miles more to cross Murphy Brook. In this vicinity, there is a road over private land that intersects the railroad. The road is not posted, but it is barred to vehicular access most of the year. Except in hunting season, it is possible to use it to reach the railroad.

To find the southern end of this local snowmobile route along the railroad, drive north on the Jerseyfield Road to the bridge over Murphy Brook, 1.3 miles north of Curtis, well south of the blue line that delineates the Park. Up the rise, beyond the brook, there is a dirt road forking right. Note that there is a similar dirt road just north of a much smaller tributary of Murphy Brook, 0.2 mile south of the brook. The Murphy Brook Road goes 1.6 miles east along the creek, but generally out of sight of it, to an attractive log hunter's camp called "Leipzig." In the late nineteenth century, Alfred Dolge had a work camp here and facilities for entertaining visitors to his piano factory. At present, the owner does not object to travel on this road when the chain is not up, but it is private land, so this could change.

The road is maintained as far as the camp. It continues north of east along the brook, joining as it goes the right of way of the old railroad, which has come from the south and Curtis. You see the embankment of the old stream crossing at the end of the road along Murphy Brook. Shortly beyond, there are signs reading "No trespassing, City of Little Falls Watershed Area." Do not stray off the track in this area.

The track swings northeast, then north 0.4 mile from Murphy Brook. Here it passes a fork for a railroad spur to the east. (This section has not been cleared recently, so you will probably not notice it.) In the next 0.2 mile, the snowmobile route crosses the edge of two marshes, the first to the west and then a somewhat larger one extending to the east with the

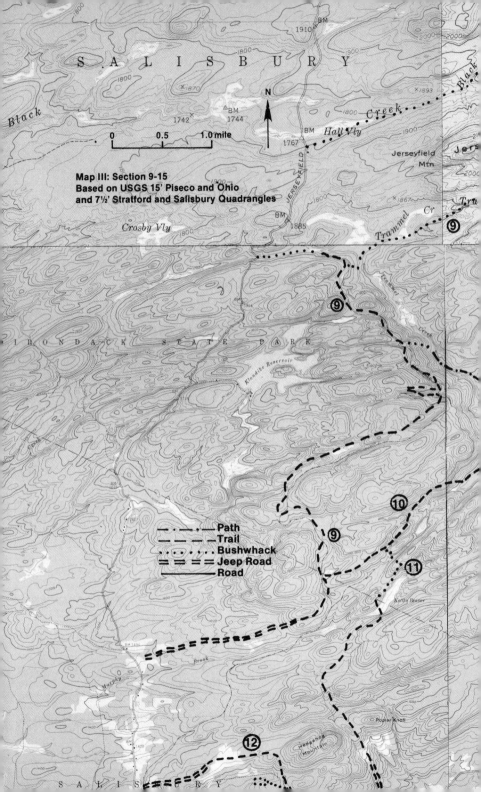

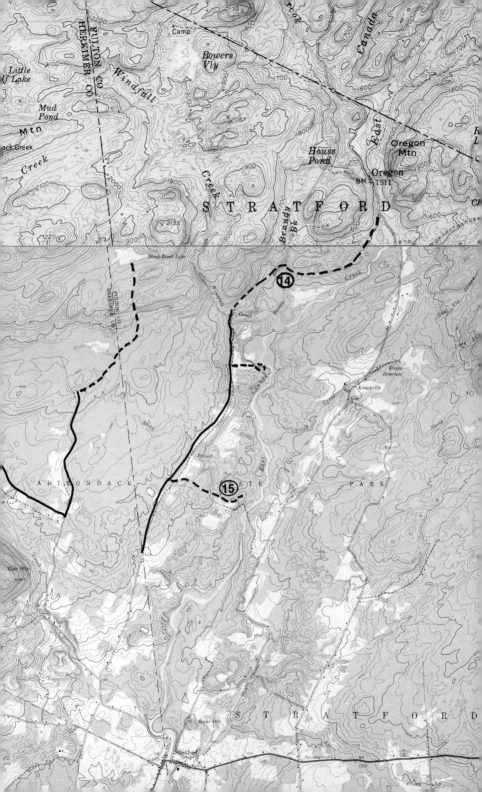

railroad on an embankment. Just beyond the embankment, there is a junction with an old white-painted, rusted metal sign pointing east to Bungtown Road, north of Stratford, section 13, and straight ahead to Klondike. The main route continues north, then northeast along the main bed of the railroad, becoming the route described above. The middle portion offers little interest for hikers, and cross-country skiers will have little trouble with this portion, especially if snowmobiles have already broken trail. Snowmobilers call it "riding the ridge" for the way it hugs the sinuous ridge above Trammel Creek.

The entire route described is nearly 9 miles long and although the grades are easy, it is too long to ski from any one point. It is suggested that you explore the route in stages from each end.

10 Murphy Brook to Bungtown
Hiking, cross-country skiing, local snowmobile route
3 miles, 1½ hours, relatively level

From Camp Leipzig, described in section 9, walk or ski to the intersection described and take the right fork, which leads through a low pass in the ridge extending north of Oak Mountain to the Bungtown Road on Trammel Creek, section 13. The first half is an almost completely unmarked route, generally clear, but indistinct in two crucial spots. It climbs only 100 feet in elevation to an attractive small lake, then the eastern half follows a dirt road down a very gradual descent of 200 feet. This is a fine trip for cross-country skiers, especially since snowmobilers make a clear track through spots that can be confusing in summer.

Leaving the intersection, the Bungtown route does not follow any railroad bed for the first 0.2 mile. It heads east on a cut through the woods on the north side of the marsh you just crossed on the railroad embankment. It then veers northeast to merge at 0.2 mile with a spur of the railroad, which continues north of east on level ground for 0.6 mile with a marsh to the south of the track all the way.

Here the track ends abruptly, and a path, hard to find and somewhat overgrown, heads southeast to cross a small stream. Continue southeast, now climbing briefly 100 yards to a sign, one way pointing to Kettle Beaver, section 11, the other to Bungtown along the continuing trail, which is once again an easily discernible route. The Bungtown route now turns

Trammel Creek

northeast straight through a draw between two low hills for 0.4 mile to a lake. Cross on the beaver dam to find a cabin on private land and a roadway on the north side. The route now follows a passable jeep trail (James Road) northeast down the valley to the Bungtown Road.

11 Kettle Beaver
Path and bushwhack

Kettle Beaver is a lovely grassy marsh three-quarters of a mile long on the border of the Adirondack Park. Murphy Brook, sometimes called Kettle Brook on old maps, flows through it. Parts of the Kettle are on watershed property and parts on state land. The meadow is older and more stable than most in the Adirondacks, with no standing dead trees and little vegetation except meadow grass. It lends itself both to hiking or to cross-country skiing.

There are two ways to reach it. From the sign described above on the trail to Bungtown, you can bushwhack 0.3 mile south over a low ridge to the meadow. James Road did once follow this route but this section is obliterated.

The second approach is from the south and James Road northeast of Salisbury Center. The first 0.7 mile of James Road can be driven, but the route is steep and rutted. You can park at Woods Corner or just past a fork in the road. Continue northeast. James Road levels off at 1 mile in a stretch that is rutted and usually wet between two small hills, Hedgehog Mountain and Poplar Knoll. The road descends to cross a small stream flowing from the west, ascends another rise and descends to the northeast to reach the Kettle Beaver Club on the banks of a tributary of Murphy Creek. James Road continues north across the creek, though the way is less obvious. It becomes a lovely woods walk as it winds northeast for 0.7 mile to the south edge of Kettle Beaver, 100 yards east of the beaver dam at the meadow's western end.

While this makes a good hiking route and a lovely ski trip, portions of this route may be posted, limiting the possibility of access to Kettle Beaver from the south.

12 Curtis to the Old Iron Mine and Irondale
Old road, cross-country skiing, exploring

Iron mining sites dot the eastern Adirondacks, but only one mine is documented in the southwestern Adirondacks. The site lies just south of the Blue Line and north of Salisbury Center. This bed of magnetic oxide was discovered in 1839, and in the 1860s iron was hauled to forges in Little Falls in the Mohawk Valley. In the first years of this century, the abandoned shafts were reopened. Captain William H. Switzer raised more than a million dollars for the Salisbury Steel and Iron Company. A mile-long tramway was built from the northwest to bring ore to the processing facilities in Irondale, on Irondale Road north of Salisbury Center. The railroad went into full-scale operation on completion of a spur connecting Irondale and Salisbury Center to the Dolgeville and Little Falls Railroad in 1909, with Captain Switzer observing from a large "Mansion House" overlooking Irondale.

Captain Switzer died in 1913 and the operation, like others in the Adirondacks, could not compete in cost with those of the Midwest. The mine closed and the state took over the property before the end of the decade. All the works were dismantled and removed, but the region, though overgrown, still reveals clues to the iron mining past.

There are two routes to the mine. An old road, which once served the mine as well as several farm sites, runs between Curtis and Fairview Corners, near Irondale. From the road junction at Curtis, take the Fuller Road east. This road was known as Blind Pig Road. Local lore holds that a farmer kept a blind pig, but there is evidence that a tavern also bore that name. Stone fences line the road and mark off old fields.

You can park within a few hundred feet of Curtis, or, with a four-wheel-drive vehicle, continue for 0.8 mile to the east and northeast and park where a faint track continues ahead through tall grass and the main track veers to the right. There has been some recent logging along this track, which heads almost straight and a little north of east for about 0.7 mile, crossing a small brook and then a somewhat larger intermittent tributary of Cold Brook. The road takes a southerly direction and heads south for 0.4 mile to a log staging area.

The road, now called Switzer Road, continues downhill a little east of south for 0.4 mile from this clearing to Fairview Corners. You can drive to this point from Salisbury by taking Curtis Road. It begins just east of where NY 29A terminates at NY 29. After 0.3 mile, bear right on Irondale Road for 1.2 miles to a cluster of homes and tiny Dolgeville Reservoir, which are all that remain of Irondale. The pavement ends here and another 0.5 mile brings you to the sharp bend in the road, which is Fairview Corners.

This through route makes a good cross-country ski route, but while hiking you will want to extend your explorations into some of the mine area. To find it, start at Fairview Corners. The road climbs for 0.2 mile and on the west side at this point, tall trees and brush conceal the foundations of the old Switzer mansion.

At 0.4 mile, the road reaches the log staging area. Here a faint track heads west becoming less and less distinguishable. You may want to do your exploring here in spring—there is a wealth of wildflowers, especially painted trillium. Further, it is easier to spot the mine relics before full leaf-out. Watch for a hundred-foot-long, five-foot mound of tailings to the left of the track. To the right, there is a small pit opening that is fenced off. Other mounds reveal themselves as tailings. Just beyond the large mound is the first of the concrete pylons on which the tramway was mounted. You can follow that line of pylons down into the creek valley. There are foundations and other clues to the mine site along the way.

The main pits, surrounded by barbed wire and definitely dangerous, lie to the northwest. You may be able to discover the roadway that leads from the mine site west to intersect the road from Curtis near the point it reaches high ground 0.8 mile from Curtis. It is possible to walk safely along this route, but do not leave it to explore the mine openings, which are deep trenches filled with water. The original shaft was 150 feet deep, a later one sixty feet deep. The main shaft branched into tunnels running east and west along the vein of ore. Both tunnels filled with water, making it necessary to pump them out.

The valley is especially handsome since the forest contains such giant black cherry trees that you will marvel at the fact the mine existed less than seventy years ago.

North of Stratford

THE COMMUNITY OF Stratford straddles the East Canada Creek and is reached from both the east and west by NY 29A. Besides the backcountry haunts known to local people, adventures from this region include a portion of the Fulton County snowmobile trail system.

13 Trammel Creek
Path, skiing, hiking, fishing
1.5 miles, 1 hour, relatively level

Trammel Creek is one of the loveliest in the area—remote and quiet, visited only by a few fishermen. A path through the valley makes it easy to explore the stream. To find the path, drive northwest on Cemetery Road from Stratford, starting at the bridge on NY 29A over the East Canada Creek, the site of the first tannery here. Take the first right fork, cross Trammel Creek, and in 0.2 mile, take a left fork, crossing the creek two more times. This road winds north to a fork, 3 miles north of Stratford. Perkins Mill Road continues straight ahead, and Bungtown Road is the left fork. This becomes a seasonal-use road and you will have to park in 1.5 miles where there is a No Motorized Vehicles sign, being careful not to block any driveways, and continue on foot or skis.

You start out to the northeast with Trammel Creek downhill on your left. You immediately cross a small intermittent stream and within ten minutes a second stream. You can see Oak Mountain through the trees to the west. Notice the huge, straight black cherry trees in the valley. Within twenty minutes, the path leads to Trammel Creek, where you can cross to some lovely picnic rocks. The path does something confusing north of these ledges. It crosses the creek to an island, continues north through the middle of the island, and then crosses the western branch of the creek. Just after you cross to the west bank, notice a large erratic. On the return this will be your clue to look for the stream crossings.

Now the valley narrows, with steep hills forming on both sides, and a small gorge lines the creek. The path crosses and recrosses the creek again within a distance of just 100 feet.

Old Farm near Edick Road

Beyond, the path leaves the creek. You will pass a cellar hole on the left, then head down into an open field with a campsite. Huge iron bars indicate the railroad once reached this clearing, some say from the heights above, section 9, but that conjecture is as confounding as it is hard to validate. Fishermen continue upstream from here, but there is no longer a clear path along the creek.

In this vicinity, there is another destination you might want to explore. Stony Brook Lake can be reached from the end of Perkins Mill Road. Go past Christian Camp to find a path that leads east to a hunting camp, then north to Stony Brook Lake. The marshes along its outlet are especially handsome.

14 Edick Road to Oregon

Snowmobile trail, good walking, cross-country skiing
1.5 miles, 40 minutes, 100-foot vertical rise

This short segment of the Fulton County Snowmobile Trail System leads from Stratford to the Powley-Piseco Road, whose haunts are described in *Discover the (Southern) Adirondacks II*. It is a delightful, smooth walk along a wide old road. If the weather has been dry, the foot tread is great— muddy spots develop in wet weather, however. And, like many other nearby snowmobile trails, this one invites skiers as long as they give way to the machines.

Drive 5 miles north of Stratford to the end of Edick Road and park in the marked area. Cross the bridge over Windfall Creek and climb the hill. In 0.1 mile you pass a building, and the continuing way is barred to all motorized vehicles except snowmobiles. The steep section continues for no more than another 0.1 mile, and for the rest of the way, grades should not give even a novice skier any trouble.

The route continues relatively level, crossing a small stream, then Brandy Brook, both on bridges. There is a slight ascent before the trail makes the long, gradual descent to the 6.4-mile mark north of Stratford on the Powley-Piseco Road, just north of the bridge over the East Canada Creek.

To extend an outing in this area, you drive back south along Edick Road for 0.4 mile to a turnout on the east side of the road. (The turnout is 4.6 miles north of Stratford.) From here a dirt road leads through a handsome plantation of mature red and white pines to a bluff above the East Canada Creek. A faint path continues along the bluff as it descends to creek level. Fishermen and picnickers enjoy this place and the sheltered roadway makes a brief, but pleasant, 0.4-mile loop to and along the creek.

15 Edick Road to Old Farm Clearing
Old road, birding, short walk
0.7 mile, 15 minutes, relatively level

A second track leads from Edick Road back toward the East Canada Creek. This one starts 3.2 miles north of the bridge in Stratford. It heads east along a small brook, then through second-growth forests to abandoned fields where only mosses and lichens have gained a footing in the sand barrens. Birds, butterflies, and berries abound. The road continues beside the field, downhill for 0.3 mile to a bridge across the creek. The continuing road leads in 0.6 mile to the Powley-Piseco Road.

Fourmile Creek

East and South of NY 8

NY 8 IS the main route north from Utica into the heart of the Adirondacks. After leaving Poland and arcing south of Hinckley Reservoir, the highway turns east to follow the West Canada Creek to Nobleboro. The story of the towns along the road—places like Hoffmeister, Morehouseville, and Wilmurt—are told in David Beetle's book, *West Canada Creek.* Their history is basically the story of their roads, the people who carried lumber to market along them, the people who worked on the roads, the taxes that supported the roads, and those who drove along them in the '20s and '30s, looking for vacations on the fringes of the wilderness. Some winter night before you venture on these roads, read Beetle's book. Then start exploring.

Hiking trails east and south of NY 8 are nonexistent. There are a number of paths and snowmobile trails, but in summer, the hiker would be totally unaware of their existence. The local ranger takes down the signs marking snowmobile trails after the winter season. He gives two reasons: The signs would be destroyed anyway and several trails cross private lands.

This problem of crossing private lands, the need for access, is more acutely felt here than in almost any other region of the Park. Additional accesses to state land may be purchased in the next few years, but their absence makes writing about this area very difficult. If you drive north on the Gray-Wilmurt Road, which parallels NY 8, you cross four roads that lead through private land, in general without reaching state land. They lead in turn to logging roads that are used by local people as ski or snowmobile routes in winter. The Town of Ohio has marked some as snowmobile trails, and a few years ago it tried to establish a system of ski routes.

Access remains a matter of local custom, and it is often possible to use these roads, so this guide will mention them briefly. A few lead to remarkably beautiful vlies. Some are loops, others interconnected with so many side roads that someone who very much enjoys skiing in the area remarked that it was often possible to keep going all day without retracing your route and still end up back at your car.

If these routes are not posted, then with a road atlas and the Ohio Quadrangle of the USGS and a compass you might enjoy exploring them on skis. None, however, start on public land.

The first is a loop that connects the two branches of Christman Road. An extension of the southerly route leads to Lafe Hall Clearing, section 3, while the northern route extends to Thorp and Twin vlies. There are logging roads that lead from Unclemeir Road up the valley of Little York Stream. Wilmurt Corners is the intersection of Atwood Road and the Gray-Wilmurt Road, sometimes called the Wilmurt Road. A road that starts on private land just over a mile south of Wilmurt Corners quickly reaches state land, crosses a private inholding, and ends at Little York Vly.

16 Ohio Gorge and Fourmile Brook
Fishing

The only way these two beautiful places can currently be enjoyed is by fishermen who obtain permits from either the Utica Boys' Club which owns them, or from the DEC offices in Utica or Herkimer. The lands are being managed under Fish and Wildlife Management Area agreement. The owners have been concerned about abuses to the properties, but do grant limited access to them. The beautiful area around the falls is posted against swimming, picnicking, and camping. This is the sort of land that the state's Environmental Quality Bond Act monies should purchase, and hopefully, the state will acquire them in the future, making it possible for all to walk along the handsome shoreline and enjoy the turbulent water of this great river.

Wilmurt Road joins NY 8 just below the falls on the West Canada Creek. If you drive south on Wilmurt Road you first cross Fourmile Brook, then drive along the West Canada where fishermen can enjoy its waters to the head of the gorge. Downstream sheer rock walls rise thirty to forty feet above the creek for a distance of nearly half a mile. It is unfortunate that the shores of the West Canada at the head of the gorge and beside the waterfall are off-limits to picnickers—they are really special places.

The lower reaches of Fourmile Brook are open to the public under the same FWMA agreement. A woods road follows the south shore of the brook upstream for 0.5 mile through an incredibly lovely valley filled with stately hemlock. Atwood Lake, in the heart of the Boys' Club property, is also open to fishermen under permit, but only from April 1 through the first Friday in June and in the month of September.

17 Upstream on Fourmile Brook
Paths, fishing, hiking

One of the prettiest spots for exploring or fishing is along unmarked paths that lead to the upper reaches of Fourmile Brook. The paths begin on a road that serves several private camps. Property along the lower end of the road is currently being logged and there are rumors that it may be sold to the state. The road, which is a new route built after the Jones Creek bridge was washed out, begins from Atwood Road, 1.5 miles east of Wilmurt Corners.

If the gate is unlocked and the weather has been dry, it is possible to drive the first 1.5 miles to within a half mile of state land. It is recommended that you walk the road, not straying from it until you reach state land. The road parallels Fourmile Brook and reaches a bridge over a tributary of the brook in 0.7 mile. The old road enters on the left just beyond the bridge. The road now traverses the log staging area for a distance of 0.5 mile, then passes two camps that back up to state land near Fourmile Brook, and reaches state land at 1.5 miles.

From here on, only hikers and fishermen have used the old logging road that continues east on high ground above the creek. At 2 miles, about a ten-minute walk beyond the last cabin, the roadway makes a distinct turn to the right. Currently a huge deadfall blocks the roadway here. If you jog around it to the east, you cross a very small stream. A wonderful fisherman's path begins on the far side of the stream. It angles downhill, northeast toward the creek and follows it more or less clearly for about 1.2 miles. You can follow this path to connect with the old road, thus making a loop walk.

Note that at the point where the path begins, you could also strike out downhill, directly north, and reach Fourmile Brook just below its confluence with Twomile Brook, which is said to be an excellent trout stream.

The roadway winds south, uphill, then continues east on a level course. It crosses two streams before reaching an intersection at 3.3 miles that is marked only with an old gas can from logging days. Continue ahead on the main road (right fork), which gradually winds downhill, reaching a bluff above Fourmile Brook in the middle of its big bend to the south. Richards Vly is 0.5 mile upstream. On the hill across the brook, east, nearer the vly, is an old lean-to shanty. This lean-to is shown on some sportsman's maps and some lists, but it is not an official DEC structure.

Even this far upstream, Fourmile Brook is a fair-sized stream, for it drains Bochen Lake and Hurrell Vly far to the east, section 21. It is also a very handsome brook, so you will enjoy discovering the fisherman's paths along its banks.

A faint path continues east along the vly, the old roadway swings west, downstream, along the brook; it becomes here just a beautiful footpath, back from the water, through deep, ferny woods. In 0.5 mile, the path reaches a small stream. Here the other arm of the roadway loops back up

Parker Vly

to the intersection, but it is so overgrown and full of blowdowns that it is difficult to follow. The path continues west along the brook, and even where it is not easy to follow, you find you are never far from its lovely course, except along the deeper bends. In 0.7 mile, the path reaches the bend in the old roadway, completing the loop.

18 Jones Road

Skiing, exploring

The eastern 3.3 miles of Jones Road is unplowed in winter. It is used then as a snowmobile trail and it makes delightful skiing. A long series of marshes and vlies begins just south of the road not far from its eastern end, and these are fun to explore on skis.

In summer, this cool woods road is a good place to walk for those who enjoy one-track dirt roads. And in summer you will find two informal paths leading south from the road toward Jones Creek and its vlies. Both are inviting.

Jones Road is the east fork, a left turn, as you cross the West Canada Bridge south of NY 8 on the Gray-Wilmurt Road. It continues southeast for 1 mile, then turns left, northeast, and in 0.3 mile reaches state land.

The eastern end of the road is 1.3 miles east of the NY 8 bridge over the West Canada at Nobleboro.

Beginning at the eastern end, Jones Road follows high ridges, possibly eskers, through deep woods. At 0.7 mile, the first of the vlies is visible off to the south, left. It is always fun to watch for birds from the edge of a vly, but the best time to enjoy one is in winter. On skis you can travel the level surface, darting around clumps of tall spruce and balsam. Stumps and snags of trees form a sculpture garden in the snow. Wind swirls and piles the snow into glittering waves. And you can reach places that can never be explored the rest of the year.

Continuing west on Jones Road, you find at 0.9 mile a turnout on the south that marks the beginning of one of the footpaths. It leads south along the marsh, though generally out of sight of it, reaching Jones Creek in 0.4 mile. The path does continue south of Jones Creek, becoming fainter and fainter as it heads into the high marsh country to the south.

West of the first path, Jones Road begins to climb. Along the entire route, it has a closed canopy of tall trees—mostly maple, which color wonderfully in fall. At 2 miles, there is a second turnout on the south. This also leads to Jones Creek near the southern end of the long marshes that surround its headwaters. This path leads east of south, downhill, into an abandoned field filled with brambles. The path winds through the field and down to a beaver pond where the path ends abruptly. Beaver have made the strangest, long, sinuous dam to create this pond. Here, too, the path continues south of the brook crossing toward Twomile Brook, but the beaver have temporarily made following it impossible. However, it is easy to walk downstream, following the stream into the deep valley, which lies in an almost east-west direction. This is a pretty and remote place, visited by very few people.

Jones Road continues southwest, climbing for another 0.8 mile before it drops fairly steeply to the intersection. Skiers will enjoy this route as well as a return, traveling from west to east, taking advantage of this short, sharp climb, and the long, easy glide back to NY 8.

19 West Canada Creek
Path, fishing, picnicking, camping

One of the rare treats in the Adirondacks is to find an undeveloped stretch of stream or river with no road along it, and a good path beside it. One of the nicest of such paths exists along the south shore of the West Canada

Creek beginning at the Nobleboro Bridge and continuing west. The path, like all fisherman's routes, is full of blowdowns and gradually disappears, but not before it leads past several good campsites.

The path begins in a small field on the south side of NY 8, just east of the bridge. It follows the shore, at first at water level, then high on the hemlock-covered banks. The mature woods offer a nice place to picnic above the water. The path seems to disappear in the vicinity of the gravel-covered island and the deep bend in the river, but you can easily make your way east to even more secluded spots.

20 Parker Vly Snowmobile Trail
Cross-country skiing

A snowmobile trail connects the eastern end of Jones Road with French Road, generally paralleling NY 8. While the trail itself has limited interest for skiers and hikers, its western end gives access to Parker Vly and a long series of marshes along Vly Brook. It is only 0.3 mile from the trailhead to the snowmobile bridge over Vly Brook, and if the marshes are well frozen, you can spend several hours skiing south and west along them. There is little flow in the brook, but watch out for open spots. When deep snows cover the grassy plain that surrounds this tiny brook, a pleasant winter trip invites. If the route seems too short, combine it with explorations along the eastern end of Jones Road, section 18.

The forest cover along the trail is especially handsome, and in summer you can walk the snowmobile trail to the vly and beyond. However, in places the trail is very wet.

21 French Road to Bochen Lake and Hurrell Vly
Snowmobile trail, hiking, skiing
4.2 miles, 2 hours, 600 foot-cumulative elevation change

This is the northern portion of the Mounts Creek Snowmobile Trail, section 3. There is a 2-mile section connecting them that is currently not cleared to make it suitable for either hiking or skiing all the way through. Should clearing be done, the trail would continue south beyond the portion described here to a sharp turn to the west to intersect the southern portion. Since this has not been walked, the desirability of a through route

Vly South of Hurrell Vly

can only be surmised. It has been reported that some snowmobiles make the through trip each winter.

In any event, there is enough of interest in the northern portion to delight the hiker or the skier. The trail begins inauspiciously and unmarked 1.3 miles south of Morehouseville on French Road, as you drive from that road's western intersection with NY 8. The beginning is an overgrown old road that is almost invisible beside a trailer and a camp. Push south through weeds and wet holes for 200 feet to discover snowmobile trail markings and a good trail.

The trail heads south for 0.25 mile to a bridge over a small stream. As the trail turns toward the southwest, it begins to climb along the west side of an unnamed hill. The trail crosses two very small streams and at 1.1 miles reaches a height of land, 400 feet above the start. As you begin to descend, now in a southerly direction, notice the lovely rock ledge to your right. A small stream follows the trail on the west and you cross it on a smooth rock outcrop. Below on your left, the stream drops into a small wetland. The forest, which to this point has been mixed hardwood, now has a number of spruce. Notice two giants beside the trail, one of which is over eight feet in circumference at breast height.

The trail now descends more steeply, and an open wet area becomes visible through the trees to the east. You will see a benchmark on a rock

Map IV: Sections 18-20, 22-28
Based on USGS 15' Ohio Quadrangle

Path
Trail
Bushwhack
Jeep Road
Road

0   0.5   1.0 mile

Twin Lakes

Twin Lakes Inlet

Wells Vly

Burp Lake

Black Creek Lake

Big

Round Top

TRAIL Stream

Twin Lakes Marsh

Crosby Vly

N

BM 1908

23

Lawson Top

North Branch Lake

Middle Branch Marsh

Branch

A   D   I   R   O

Cotton Lake

Middle   A   Creek

BM 2031

JEEP

Mill Creek Lake

BM 1701

Mill

TRAIL

24

Mad Tom Lake

BM 1753

Black

JEEP

O   H   I   O

28

Mad Tom Brook

McCauley Mtn

1472

Pooler Vly

Swan Lake

27

White Lead Lake

Bullhead Pond

CREEK

BM

Wilmurt

in the middle of the trail. Beyond, the trail traverses a small rise and descends to the outlet of Bochen Lake and the beginning of Hurricane Brook at 1.6 miles, a forty-five-minute walk. A dam once held back a nearly mile-long body of water that is now mostly a grassy vly, though a beaver dam to the east now holds back a small area of open water.

Beyond a second bridge, the outlet is split. The trail climbs again, quickly leveling out and heading generally south. For the next mile, it crosses level ground and innumerable wet areas. One spruce swamp may be difficult to cross, with standing water in the trail and on both sides of it. At 2.9 miles, the trail begins to descend and a small stream forms to the right of the trail. The trail turns southwest and hugs the side of a hill, descending more steeply to cross the stream and follow it briefly. The trail now turns west and drops to Hurrel Vly at 3.4 miles. This portion of the walk should take fifty minutes. The vly is a large grass meadow, and concealed in the high grass is a good bridge over Hurrell Brook, which flows through the vly. You will find the bridge about 100 feet to the west of the point the trail reaches the vly.

Across the bridge, there is no trail through the meadow, but you can see a snowmobile trail marker directly south. It leads to a short rise. The trail, heading west of south, becomes filled with witch hobble. Fifteen minutes will suffice for the 0.5-mile walk to the next stream crossing, this one at the end of another long series of grassy vlies.

You can continue south for a short distance more before being stopped by numerous blowdowns, but this might be a good place to turn around. If you are on skis, you can explore all the vlies you cross, particularly the meadows that fill Bochen Lake, and you will enjoy the long, gentle run downhill from the height-of-land north of Hurricane Brook.

Black River Wild Forest

FOR A CENTURY, logging reigned supreme in the area now known as the Black River Wild Forest. Settlements bordering on the west have such names as Forestport and Woodgate. Today, the region is a mixture of maturing second-growth forests and stands that have been recently logged; but the mature forests dominate. The wildness of the days before the loggers again pervades.

The Black River Wild Forest is a land of large, southwest-flowing creeks and rivers that break it into distinct smaller regions. The Middle Branch of the Moose River bounds the north; the South Branch, Bear, Woodhull, and Little Woodhull creeks, and the Black River traverse the region.

This is a large region, with numerous private inholdings. It is bounded on the west by the Blue Line of the Adirondack Park and on the east by the Adirondack League Club. That club was founded in 1890, two years before the creation of the Park, by a group of men whose principal interest was a private hunting, fishing, and recreation preserve.

As with many private preserves founded near the end of the nineteenth century, this one owes its origin to the railroads, which made travel to the deep Adirondack interior possible. And like other preserves, this one rankled and upset the natives and guides who had fished and hunted freely in the region, for the entire area was posted. Today all the club's holdings remain closed to the public.

Though the club holds or leases less than 100,000 acres today, it comprised over 200,000 acres shortly after its founding, and of these 93,000 were covered with virgin forest. The members dedicated the club to the preservation and conservation of Adirondack forests, the proper protection of game and fish, an improved system of forestry, and the maintenance of an ample preserve for its members' enjoyment. Club lands contained Honnedaga, Bisby, and Little Moose lakes as well as sixty smaller lakes and ponds. North Lake Road, the only route to the Honnedaga portion of the preserve, is a prominent access to some of this guide's adventures.

The Black River Wild Forest has been called the great abused wilderness. It is certainly a wild and desolate region, one that appeals to those who want solitude. Even though it is bisected by North Lake Road, these attributes and the size of the portions meet the State Land Master Plan's definition of Wilderness. An equal case can be made demonstrating that it has been abused. Trails in the south are not maintained, though those in the north near the Nicks Lake Campground seem to receive the finest care. Motorized vehicles have to be permitted on some of the roads that lead to private inholdings, but so much of the area is currently used illegally by all-terrain vehicles that many of the trails are in very bad shape. As new legislation addresses the trespass of these vehicles on state land, the trails will once again be the peaceful routes to distant lakes that hikers, fishermen, cross-country skiers, and snowmobilers enjoy.

However, if you are willing to walk several miles, this region offers many remote and undisturbed ponds, lakes, and miles of river shore. There are a few lovely waterfalls and enough quiet trails so that you will almost always see wildlife. And you will meet far fewer people than in the popular Wilderness areas of the Park.

Mill Creek Lake

Haskell Road

HASKELL ROAD, OR Haskell Lane as it used to be called, follows the West Canada Creek north from Nobleboro for 9 miles to a gate at private land. The first 2.5 miles are graded and easy to drive; the last 6.5 are a challenge for any four-wheel-drive vehicle even though the bridges are at present in good repair. There are two large private inholdings along the way and several smaller ones surrounding hunting camps. You will find numerous turnouts where campers have stopped, for more than ninety percent of the land along the road is in the Forest Preserve. There are few such roads in the Adirondacks where travel by jeep or pickup is not prohibited and where the terrain is so handsome.

Perhaps it is peculiar that a hiking guide mention the driveability of a wild dirt road, but there are times when walking the road is less than desirable. The rocks and ruts are less frequent than a few years ago, but lake-sized mud puddles span the roadway and make walking difficult. The driving would be difficult as well if it were not for the fact that there is something of a firm gravel base beneath the wet sections of road.

Skiing the road in winter is delightful, however, and highly recommended.

Places to look for on the way north include a road toward the creek at 0.5 mile north of the bridge at Nobleboro. This right, east, fork branches again and both portions lead to campsites near the river. At 1.4 miles north on Haskell Road there is a parking turnout on a bluff high above the creek; below there is a spring and a campsite on a hemlock-covered bank. At 1.5 miles there is a path left, section 22. The first large private inholding spans the road around 2.7 miles. This posted section is just above the junction of Betty Green Creek at the head of the rapids with the same name. In the next half mile, there are several places to pull off the road, which is high above but close to the creek. At two of these, paths lead to creekside; but the northern leads to a cable crossing that gives access to a private inholding on the east bank. Downstream from the crossing is a particularly choice spot with a deep flume and potholes carved into the granite base of the creek. At 3.6 miles, the snowmobile trail to Little Salmon Lake forks left. There is a bridge at 3.7 miles and a larger bridge over Big Brook at 3.9 miles. Several good campsites are located north of the second bridge.

The road really becomes questionable north of this point, especially where it is close to the Seabury Stillwater. Here, the last of the large logging camps on the river was located. At 5.4 miles you pass Seabury Brook and a camp. At 7.9 miles the road crosses Jones Brook and the path for Honnedaga Falls, section 26, begins here. Just north is the confluence with Metcalf Brook. Fishing is reported to be especially good in the next mile of stream south of the gated property.

The area around Nobleboro was logged in 1790 when Arthur Noble rafted logs down the West Canada to the Mohawk and west to Albany where they were loaded on ships that sailed to Ireland. Farming and lumbering continued on a small scale throughout the next century, but it was not until the 1890s that the forests around the West Canada were heavily logged. In the decade of the '90s, dams were built at three stillwaters on the river to create surges to float logs downstream. Hundreds of loggers were employed in the woods and river drivers risked blasting the jams and riding logs through the rapids. If you are serious about discovering this region, read tales of the logging days in Harvey Dunham's *French Louie* to match the exploits of both trappers and loggers to sites along the river.

22 Mill Creek Lake and Lookout

Abandoned snowmobile trail, old road, bushwhack, lookout
3.2 miles, 2 hours to lake, 5.1 miles, 2¾ hours to lookout,
400-foot vertical rise

There are several obstacles to overcome in getting to Mill Creek Lake. Even though most of the shoreline is state-owned, it is either boggy or densely wooded. The most accessible shore is on the south, but it is privately owned and has some camps. The southern approach is confused by the fact the dirt road leading to the inholdings from NY 8 begins on private land. Therefore, other than a bushwhack, the only way to reach the lake without infringing on the land owner's rights is a lengthy hike on a snowmobile trail from Hooper Dooper Road past Mad Tom Lake, section 28, or along the route of the abandoned snowmobile trail described here. It is not an easy trail to follow. In addition to the absence of maintenance, there are many abrupt direction changes that seem to be unnecessary. Markers are usually near at hand, and if you temporarily lose the trail, careful, methodical searching and attention to direction should enable you to continue. However, since it does not constantly follow an old road grade and any sign of a path is not continuous, it is only a matter of time before natural forces obscure the route.

The trail begins on the northwest side of Haskell Road, 1.5 miles from

NY 8. There is still enough room for two or three cars to park, even though the turnout is beginning to grow in. A sign cautions that the only motorized vehicles permitted are snowmobiles. The beginning of the route is along an old logging road that ascends to the north, then swings west through a coniferous section where a herd path leads left to a clearing higher up on the hillside. The grade levels off and in twenty minutes you cross a stream, then recross it where former bridges now lie rotting. The trail begins to get wet and you cross a second, larger stream on a long plank bridge that is rotting and very slippery. Heading north-northwest, you pass through a very wet section, then turn west, paralleling the stream flowing just out of sight on your left.

After half an hour, you reach a section where beech and viburnum are filling in the trail. Gradually swinging north, it opens up as it begins to ascend. There are a few red paint blazes. After turning northwest, the trail crosses a small stream and reaches another overgrown area. Red flagging and markers guide you through on a north-northwest bearing. After fifty minutes, the trail turns almost north, crosses a stream, and reaches a point where a line blazed with can covers and red paint comes in from the west. Not long afterward, the trail turns west and passes through tall hemlocks. Through the trees on your right, you see a wetland along Mill Creek and after an hour and a quarter of hiking, you cross Mill Creek on a log bridge.

Beyond the bridge, the trail turns abruptly south and goes through a small alder thicket. After a short ascent and a zigzag southeast then south, the trail makes a wide swing to the west through mixed tree cover where markers are few. A final turn south leads shortly to a dirt road, one and a half hours from the trailhead. To the right, this road leads in 0.2 mile to private land and Mill Creek Lake. Turn left onto the road and begin to ascend away from the lake. In 100 yards, the road joins the dirt road coming in from NY 8, 2 miles away. Turn right at this junction, heading west and following occasional markers.

In the next ten minutes, you will see several yellow-blazed lines and pipes on the right indicating the boundaries of private parcels. You will also pass two driveways leading to camps on the lake. Beyond the second driveway, a yellow-painted state land boundary pipe marks a borderline heading 34° magnetic. An easy five-minute bushwhack along this line will take you to the brushy shore. Patches of weeds break the water's surface; spruce, balsam, and hemlocks line its edges. Wetlands lie to the west along a major inlet and to the east near the outlet. A ridge rises steeply to the north with the wooded dome of Lawson Top behind to the right. Two rock outcrops can be seen on the ridge, and a bushwhack to the eastern one will yield extensive views across the lake and to the southeast.

Mill Creek Snowmobile Trail

A well-marked hunter's path leads west from the camps to a point on the dirt road just south of where it crosses the lake's major inlet. Can covers with the top half painted blue and the bottom painted orange follow roughly the line at which the hardwoods meet the conifers around the lake's edge, and from where you stand you should be able to see the line. To get around the lake and into a position for a bushwhack to the outcrop, you may follow this path or return along the state land boundary to the road, turn right, and follow its descent to the inlet. Either way will take about fifteen minutes, but the path is more level and interesting.

After crossing the inlet on a long plank bridge, the road leads through a dense stand of spruce and balsam. It then rises, passes an old road heading off to the right, and comes to a junction where a snowmobile trail heads west to Mad Tom Lake, section 24. You now begin a long, gradual ascent through a beautiful hardwood forest dominated by tall maples and beech. The road soon splits and you follow the right fork that leads to Black Creek Lake, section 23. Twenty minutes after crossing the inlet, you have gained 250 feet and the road levels into a wet, grassy stretch. A small stream approaches to within 15 yards on the right. Leave the road and cross the stream on a bearing of 120° magnetic east-southeast. This will take you to the ridge line. Following it east, you will come in ten minutes to a small, scrubby, bedrock summit where there are limited views through the trees. Continue east, dropping down off the summit and reaching a second high spot. After another minute's walk, head straight for the lake. The outcrop is just below you, and from the top of the rock all of Mill Creek Lake and its wetlands are visible. A ridge beyond the lake blocks views to the south, but to the southeast, the hills north of Jerseyfield Lake stretch to the horizon. Fort Noble Mountain rises to the east-southeast and behind it lies Bethune Mountain and the country surrounding the South Branch of the West Canada Creek.

23 Black Creek Lake

Old road, bushwhack
7 miles, 3½ hours, 400-foot vertical rise

Like Mill Creek Lake, Black Creek Lake's most accessible shore is on the south and is blocked by a private inholding. A bushwhack around the parcel is the only way to reach the densely wooded shoreline, but as of 1986, the boundaries are not well-defined and it is difficult to know for sure if you are on state land. Once past these obstacles, however, the backwoods explorer will appreciate the dark, quiet waters and surrounding ridges that give this lake its character. The lake is at the center of the Black River Wild Forest. Since you reach the lake with relative ease, you are in a position to take advantage of the countless opportunities for deep woods explorations.

The dirt road you follow from Mill Creek Lake, section 22, is still designated as a snowmobile trail, but it has become more rugged and there are occasional rutted, muddy areas. For one half hour after crossing the Mill Creek Lake inlet, the trail's rocky course climbs north through a mature hardwood forest. The terrain then becomes rolling, markers are rare, and a wetland is visible through the trees to the west. Following a forty-minute walk from the inlet, a distance of 2 miles, the road drops to a very wet, rutted area and crosses a stream that flows into the wetland. Just beyond, take the right fork where the road splits. You encounter more puddles, then the land rises and you see an old truck on the left.

You cross another stream and in the next five minutes see three signs. The first indicates the snowmobile trail in the direction from which you have been walking. The second says "Stop End of Snowmobile Trail." The third sign indicates the private land of the Black Creek Lake Club and warns against trespassing. You reach this boundary after an hour's walk from Mill Creek Lake inlet, and since private land extends quite far to the east, your best plan is to bushwhack west, making a wide swing north to the lake or its outlet.

24 Mad Tom Lake
Snowmobile trail, hiking, cross-country skiing
5.2 miles, 2 hours 40 minutes, 200-foot vertical rise

Mad Tom Lake can be reached from the old road to Black Creek Lake by turning left onto a snowmobile trail at a junction 0.3 mile past the Mill Creek Lake inlet, section 22. There are very few markers along this section, but snowmobiles use it regularly and all-terrain vehicles have made the route obvious in other seasons.

Heading west from the intersection through a mostly hardwood section, you cross a stream in less than ten minutes. In twenty minutes, the trail turns south and a sign indicates a junction. Ahead, the trail swings right and leads 3.7 miles to Hooper Dooper Road, section 28. Turn left and follow the trail as it descends into evergreens and out to the edge of the lake, 0.1 mile away. Mad Tom Lake is actually a small pond about three acres in size and is surrounded by a much larger shrub wetland where many tamaracks grow intermixed with dead standing timber. Sweet gale, sheep laurel, low-bush cranberries, and pitcher plants abound, but the ATVs are damaging much of the vegetation near the trail entrance.

25 Little Salmon Lake

Snowmobile trail, part bushwhack, hiking, fishing, hunting, snowshoeing

This partially abandoned snowmobile trail follows parts of the old Jocks Lake Road. Jock Wright was a trapper whose exploits were popularized by Jeptha R. Simms in his *Trappers of New York.* Jock served in the Revolutionary War and hunted and trapped throughout New England. In 1796, he moved to Norway, New York, and spent the rest of his life hunting and trapping in the headwaters region of the East and West Canada creeks. Among his favorite fishing haunts was a lake he discovered in 1805. It was known as Jocks Lake until the late nineteenth century when it was renamed Honnedaga. It has also been called Transparent Lake because of the extraordinary clarity of its deep blue waters.

Jock frequently visited both his lake and Little Salmon Lake, which lies to the south of Jocks Lake. He caught trout throughout the year to take back to settlements in the valley. In the years before he died in 1826 at the age of 75, he had a hunting cabin at Rocky Point at Jocks Lake. It is sad to note that both lakes, which lie close to 2200 feet in elevation, have been so susceptible to acid rain that today they are devoid of fish.

Logging roads were pushed towards Jocks Lake from Nobleboro to Jocks Lake in the middle of the century. Just after 1880, A. D. Barber built a hotel, Forest Lodge, near Rocky Point at Jocks Lake. Until the completion of North Lake Road, guests reached the establishment traveling by train from Utica to Prospect Station, then by stage to Wilkinson's at Nobleboro, where they spent the night and prepared for the arduous last leg of the trip. The last ten miles was over the Jocks Lake Road, "one of the worst roads in the north." The road was all "ups and downs . . . said to be uphill either way you traveled it. There were hard pulls up Town Camp and Thunder Brook Hills and past Whiskey Springs."

Today you can follow this route almost to Little Salmon Lake. Drive 3.6 miles in on Haskell Road from NY 8 at Nobleboro. The last mile is very rough and you may choose to walk it. A guideboard at the trailhead states the distance to Little Salmon Lake as 10.5 miles, South Pond, 18 miles. This sign might better be posted back on NY 8, for the distance from here to Little Salmon Lake is about 7 miles. A round trip on the trail and path with some bushwhacking to the lake will take six to seven hours.

The trail begins by heading uphill, first north, then northwest for 0.8 mile. The trail turns west, then sharply north. At 1.6 miles, the trail swings west and begins a series of ups and downs. At 2.8 miles, you reach a ce-

Mill Creek from the Cliffs

ment bridge over Big Brook. There is a USGS benchmark embedded in the bridge. Jeeps have used the trail up to this point, and you can walk it in an hour.

Beyond the bridge, the trail takes a northeasterly course following the valley of the tributary of Big Brook that drains Whiskey Spring Vly. You can see why old-timers complained about the hills; in less than 3 miles, the trail climbs 720 feet. An hour and ten minutes walking, 3.2 miles past the bridge, you reach a fork in the trail. The way right leads to a camp on a private inholding. The way left or straight ahead continues fairly obviously for almost 0.2 mile, then becomes very overgrown. There is a fork here, though it is so overgrown you may miss it.

The way left follows an old roadway and heads west to connect with old logging roads from South Lake. From this path, you have to bushwhack north to reach the lake where you will find a faint footpath along the lakeshore.

The fork to the right starts just as the trail becomes overgrown. This faint path heads north and meets the snowmobile trail again, for it seems that the snowmobile trail does not exactly follow the route of the old roads, but cuts through the clearing around the camp. North of the camp, the trail is fairly obvious as it heads downhill. In the valley, about 0.7 mile past the camp, there is a good path leading west toward the lake, though you will have to look sharply to discover the place it branches from the main route, turning left, west.

Several things have lead to the deterioration of the snowmobile trail and the confusion near the lake: few people seem to have used the bypass trail cut south of Little Salmon Lake; the distance is too great for today's trail crews to maintain trails near the lake because the crews return to base each evening; snowmobilers seem to have used the trail north, then west to the lake, probably crossing the frozen surface of the lake before returning cross-country to the trail to South Lake; and the hunters who are using the area maintain the trail north of its official designation. In fact, the trail north, following the old road to Herkimer Landing is well maintained beyond the valley at least as far as the Adirondack League Club boundary.

You can add to this already long trek a different route for the return. From the cabin site, you can bushwhack southeast to Threemile Vly, follow its outlet south to Sucker Brook, then contour west along the base of the hill past Whiskey Spring Vly, staying on this course until you meet the trail again. Portions of this trek are fairly steep for skiing, but the route lends itself to a snowshoe trek when making the return circuit through these vlies would be the easiest.

26 High Falls on Honnedaga Outlet
Bushwhack

If you are camping along the northern reaches of Haskell Road near the West Canada, this is the perfect bushwhack. Paths formerly led all the way to the falls. Since this trip was first described in *Fifty Hikes in the Adirondacks*, the state has acquired the private hunting camp on the brook, so the trail to it is no longer cared for. The route is still the same, though overgrown in many places. It is 3.6 miles each way, but the round trip from Haskell Road now requires more than five hours.

You can still see the path heading northwest along the north side of Jones Brook from a point just short of 8 miles north on Haskell Road. Follow it as it climbs beneath Beaverdam Pond and stays to high ground through a hemlock bog and a place called the rock garden. Corduroy, perhaps a century old, is your clue to the route. Just short of a mile, the path takes a due west course and begins to follow the brook closely. You may

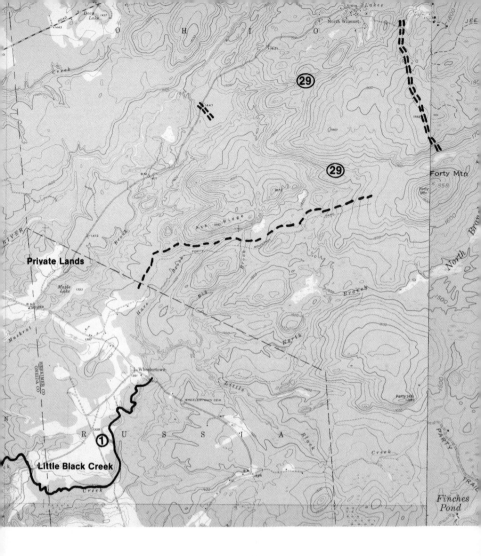

notice a fork here; your route is the left branch which stays close to the
brook. At 1.4 miles, you reach Jones Brook, just upstream from its confluence with Honnedaga Outlet, or Baby Lake Outlet as it is known locally. Head upstream for 100 feet to a ford that permits a dry, rock-hopping
crossing, except in very high water.

The path grows fainter as it follows close by Baby Lake Outlet in a northwest direction. As the outlet makes a loop to the south, the trail keeps
the same northwest direction, cutting across a hillside. Blazes mark the
route, but it has almost become a bushwhack. Just short of 1.5 miles past
the Jones Brook crossing, the path returns to the side of the brook, descending to cross it where the brook angles north. The dilapidated bridge here

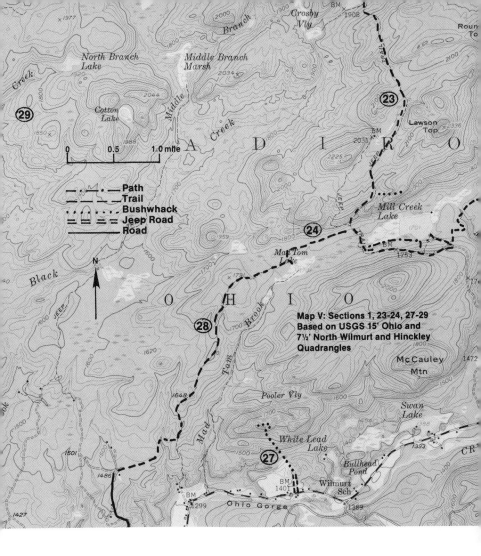

Map V: Sections 1, 23-24, 27-29
Based on USGS 15' Ohio and
7½' North Wilmurt and Hinckley
Quadrangles

may be gone, for there is no longer anyone to repair it. High Falls Camp, which stood in a field here just north of the bridge, is no more—it was burned when the state acquired the property.

There is no trace of path to lead you north from here to the falls 0.6 mile away. Do not try to follow the brook north for the marshes along it make difficult travel. Instead, bushwhack along the base of the hill that lies to the west, just high enough to avoid the flood plain. This bit of elevation will help when you try to cross the first stream you meet, for to the east is all marsh. Continue along the base of the hill to the falls, which is a double stream that cascades down nearly 90 feet from a marsh upstream on Baby Lake Outlet.

North of NY 8 and 365

MOST OF THE frontage along NY 8 and NY 365 is privately owned, and public access is greatly restricted. Several old roads lead north into the interior, but with few exceptions, they begin on private land and you should seek permission before using them. State acquisition of some parcels is now under consideration and this will greatly improve public access.

A labyrinth of old logging roads and acres of vlies invite the cross-country skier, but such exploration should be approached as wilderness ski-touring. Strong orienteering and route-finding abilities are recommended, as is a good dose of woods wisdom and common sense. Some informal snowmobile trails see seasonal use, but there are many remote corners where isolation is guaranteed and a true wilderness experience awaits.

Area woodsmen have marked a number of personal and frequently used paths and this illegal practice may be confusing to visitors who try to follow them. Internal DEC recommendations call for the improving of some snowmobile trails by rerouting and cutting new connecting links. Such changes are not imminent and will be addressed in future revisions of this guide.

27 Lookout North of NY 8
Bushwhack

In an area with precious few lookouts, it is ironic that one so easily accessible remains virtually unknown. The 0.8 mile, forty-five minute climb takes you 400 feet up this small hill to survey much of the southern portion of this guide.

NY 8 rises as it parallels the Ohio Gorge. At 2.2 miles north of its junction with NY 365, a large clearing and gravel pit are located on the left. High up on a ridge behind the clearing, a rock outcrop can be seen facing south. A driveway immediately past the entrance to the gravel pit leads 0.2 mile through a narrow strip of state land to another, smaller gravel pit. This acquisition was made as a "hunter's access" and while it is not developed, there are many places to park. The entire driveway is not plowed in winter, but there is usually a turnout near the highway where plows have winged back the snow.

Lookout above NY 8 near Ohio Gorge

From the small gravel pit the driveway turns left, then curves around to the right and you should see the yellow-blazed boundary line on your left. A grassy path enters from the left at the top of a rise and at this point you should begin a bushwhack north along the boundary line. Ten minutes from your parked vehicle, you will come to a corner pipe on the boundary. Set your compass for 350° magnetic and climb north-northwest through the hardwood cover. Fifteen minutes after crossing a stream, you should be at the base of the cliffs. Turn right and follow along the interesting outcroppings as you search for a way to ascend to the ridge line. Several possible routes will present themselves and once above the rock, follow along its top to the left, west. You will soon find a small shelf above the outcrop you spotted from NY 8.

The view south covers about 100° and to the east you look across the hills of the western edge of the Ferris Lake Wild Forest Area near the Gray-Wilmurt Road. The Dairy Hill Fire Tower, section 2, is visible on the horizon, and to its right is the needlelike Fairfield transmission tower. Closer in, you see the course of the West Canada Creek cutting through the Ohio Gorge and widening out as it flows west toward settled lands. On the horizon at your far right toward Utica, more transmission towers rise above the distant hills. In the winter, when this is a delightful snowshoe trek with deep snow and dropped leaves, you can see in other directions if you explore along the top of the ridge.

28 Mad Tom Lake from Hooper Dooper Road
Snowmobile trail, hiking, cross-country skiing
3.7 miles, 1¾ hours

This is the easiest route to Mad Tom Lake and it also provides a more visible, though longer approach to the country around Mill Creek Lake and Black Creek Lake, sections 22 through 24. Wet areas are few and there is little blowdown. Markers, though few, are there when you need them.

At a point along NY 365 less than 0.1 mile from its end at the junction with NY 8, Hooper Dooper Road branches north. Its 1.5 miles gives access to many camps and private parcels and it is plowed in winter. At 1.2 miles, just after a rise and a curve left, a snowmobile trail leaves the road from a turnout on the right where two or three cars can park. The trailhead is marked with a faded brown and yellow DEC sign and a green and yellow sign stating that motorized vehicles are prohibited except snowmobiles when conditions permit. As you might suspect, all-terrain vehicles have also driven on the trail, but so far, their impact has not been great.

The trail heads east-northeast through a level hardwood forest dominated by tall maples, beech, and birches. After fifteen minutes, a short descent takes you to a brook. You turn north and walk beside it for 0.1 mile before crossing. Beyond, the trail ascends northeast up the far bank then makes a broad swing to the southeast, intersecting an old road 0.8 mile and twenty-five minutes from the trailhead. To the right, the road descends for about 0.7 mile to private land and NY 8. The marked trail turns left onto the old road and signs at this junction point the way to Black Creek Lake as well as back to Hooper Dooper Road.

For the next fifty minutes, you will be gradually climbing over rolling and unchanging terrain as the trail winds northeast to Mad Tom Lake. Height-of-land is reached after 2.9 miles, and ten minutes later you descend to a wet area with many conifers. Five minutes later you will see a small grassy clearing on the right; it contains old parts of stoves as well as a garbage pit. You cross a stream beyond the clearing and in three minutes you reach a junction with the side trail leading right, 0.1 mile to Mad Tom Lake. A sign at this junction points left to Black Creek Lake. It is 0.8 mile further to the old road between Mill Creek and Black Creek lakes.

Farr Road

FARR ROAD WAS the original route to North Lake, starting on Bellingertown Road, southeast of Forest Port, and running northeast for 7.2 miles to Reeds Pond, section 34. Today it is a fair dirt road with several camps in the area known as North Wilmurt.

North Wilmurt used to be called Farrtown after Ed Farr and his family of three sons who ran a "hotel" there, though like most such establishments, it was little more than a roadside saloon. The Farrs were equally well known for their occupation as shingle shavers.

To reach Farr Road today, turn right at the north end of the bridge at Forestport and drive east for 1.2 miles to Forestport Station. Just before the Buffalo Head Hotel, turn right and proceed 0.7 mile to a junction with Bellingertown Road, which comes in from the left. Follow it east-southeast, crossing the Black River at 4.6 miles. The next short piece of road is given as Enos Road on the Atlas. At 5.3 miles, just past a farm on the right, Farr Road enters on the left. The approach from NY 365 is complicated since the most direct route has lost its bridge over the Little Black Creek and a lengthy detour is necessary. Follow NY 365 west from its junction with NY 8 for 7.3 miles, then turn right onto Fairchild Road. Proceed for 2.0 miles to Lake Julia Road, which enters from the right. Take this road, crossing Kayuta Reservoir on a steel-decked bridge at 4.8 miles. At 5.9 miles, Bellingertown Road enters on the right. Follow it as outlined above.

Since none of the trails in the area are very long, you might enjoy a very short canoe trip that is reached by this strange maze of roads. A tributary of the Black River, Little Black Creek, is surprisingly nice. Its steep upper section is inaccessible, but there is an attractive flatwater section in the Park and a short whitewater section just outside the Park.

The southeast fork at the intersection of Enos and Farr Roads is Wheelertown Road. Take it to the bridge over Little Black Creek and put in there. From Wheelertown Road to Hughes Road, 3 miles, the creek wanders gently through woods and marsh. It bumps against an occasional low bluff. Overall it is much prettier than the flat, sandy plain into which it is cut.

There are a few short riffles that may require stepping out at summer levels. About halfway down is a rocky riffle at the end of Spall Road, where the bridge once was. To the south 200 feet on Spall Road is a DEC park-

Floodgate at Twin Lakes Reservoir

ing area for fishermen. To the north, Spall Road is abandoned. The shores are private, but the state does have a fishing easement.

Within sight of Hughes Road, rapids begin. Land on the left at the head of the rapids and carry along a trail 150 feet to the road. Wheelertown is to the right up Hughes Road 1.7 miles, then right on Wheelertown for 0.3 mile to the beginning of the canoe trip. Wheelertown is a town no more. Not even one structure survives. The whole area has an abandoned feel, forgotten and returning to wilderness.

29 East and South of North Wilmurt
Bushwhacks, old roads, hunting

The lands belonging to the state east and south of North Wilmurt contain many ridges, streams, valleys, and vlies. For the experienced backwoods traveler, many peaceful explorations await. Three suggested access points are described here; all are in the Forest Preserve.

From the southern end of Farr Road, turn southeast onto Wheelertown Road and pass a small lake with a spillway on the left at 0.2 mile. At an intersection at 0.7 mile, bear left onto Lite Road and follow it to its end, 0.7 mile in. There is room to park here and you will notice that the road continues on as a well-defined woods road. It is possible to follow its course over 3 miles to the vicinity of Forty Mountain, a high, completely wooded hill.

As you travel north along Farr Road, a dirt road turns off into a reforested area at 2.7 miles. It leads to a campsite in 0.2 mile, and many vehicles with enough ground clearance drive into the area. A path leads from the southern edge of the site down to Muskrat Brook, 100 yards away. It continues beyond the brook into the area north of Ash Ridge.

At an intersection at the settlement of North Wilmurt, 5 miles from the south end of Farr Road and 2.2 miles from the North Lake Road, Withers Road heads east. Follow it over the top of a hill at 0.4 mile and to the top of a second hill at 0.6 mile. Here, the road bends sharply to the left and an old road heads off to the right. There is room to park at the entrance. This route can be followed south, then east into the region of the North Branch of Little Black Creek.

30 Twin Lakes

Snowmobile trail, hiking, cross-country skiing, snowshoeing,
campsites, hunting, fishing
3.2 miles, 1½ hours, 450-foot cumulative rise

The Twin Lakes basin was once dammed as part of the whole effort to regulate the flow of the Black River and its tributaries. The dam is now long gone and only a stone floodgate remains at the outlet. What was once a large, shallow reservoir, has reverted to an extensive, brushy wetland with two residual pools of water. It is a haven for wildlife who depend on this environment. Walking through the wetland is difficult and the surrounding woods is quite dense in places, so winter is the best time for a visit. Anglers, however, will brave the dampness of spring and the hordes of insects for a chance to catch some native trout.

A snowmobile trail follows the route of the old road east to the southern end of the former reservoir. It begins at a parking area on the east side of Farr Road, 0.6 mile south of its intersection with North Lake Road. The trail is barely marked and poorly maintained, having many mudholes and grown-in sections, but snowmobiles and all-terrain vehicles do push through, the latter illegally. From the trailhead register, a lengthy initial ascent takes you through mature hardwoods with occasional stands of evergreens. After half an hour, the terrain becomes rolling and ten minutes later you cross a small vly.

After an hour, a moderate descent takes you to a large vly that you must cross on old rotting logs. It is extremely wet and care is needed. Reentering the woods, you pass through a lush area of tall ferns, then rise away from the surrounding evergreens. A stream is heard, then seen as it tumbles along on your left. A rock outcrop lies to the right and the trail continues to climb, swinging right, above it. After a moderate ascent through a grown-in area, you reach the height-of-land, then drop to the edge of the lower "lake," just above the outlet. Turning right, you can hop rocks along the edge to the remains of the floodgate.

At the upper "lake" a major inlet enters from the east, and it is reportedly a good spot to fish. On the north edge of the lake, an old hunter's path enters from North Lake Road, section 36. Several campsites may be found here, but they are excessively littered with plastic sheeting, pieces of rope, fuel cans, and bottles.

Along North Lake Road

THE FIRST HALF of the nineteenth century saw the wilderness of the Black River Valley give way to intense development and colonization. The early settlers were quick to realize the river's potential, particularly at High Falls, Long Falls, and the Great Falls where Lyons Falls, Carthage, and Watertown are located today.

Textile, lumber, and paper industries, as well as the Black River Canal system, exploited the river's water but their operations were plagued by inconsistencies in the water's flow. Spring floods damaged or destroyed many mills and factories, and summer droughts not only hindered canal navigation but so curtailed water power that some industries had to adopt steam as a back-up power source. One by one, throughout the entire Black River watershed, dams were proposed and reservoirs constructed in an effort to regulate the flow. The net effect was beneficial to downstream communities, but the dam building process was slow and wrought with controversy and disaster.

Far up on the Black River, in a long valley where many streams converged, lay small Lake Sophia. The first dam built at this site on the Black River was completed in 1856, creating the North Branch Reservoir. That dam could not contain the spring floods of 1869 and the resulting torrent caused great destruction down the entire length of the river. An improved dam and spillway complex was constructed and North Lake, as we know it today, has changed little since then.

North Lake Road runs northeast through the center of the Black River Wild Forest Area and it provides access to many of the waters that received regulatory scrutiny. From the village of Forestport, turn right off NY 28 at the north end of the bridge over the Black River. Travel east for 1.2 miles through the hamlet of Woodhull to Forestport Station where the tracks of the Adirondack Railroad cross at an intersection. Ahead of you, past the Buffalo Head Hotel, North Lake Road enters the woods of the high plateau of the western Adirondack foothills. Road mileages to destinations along the way are given from the railroad tracks.

A note about winter use of the area: North Lake Road is plowed, so there is access to all the trailheads mentioned. Most of the long trails are so well cleared that they lend themselves to winter ski-touring. All the vlies are fun to explore on skis. Snowshoers will find that every route in

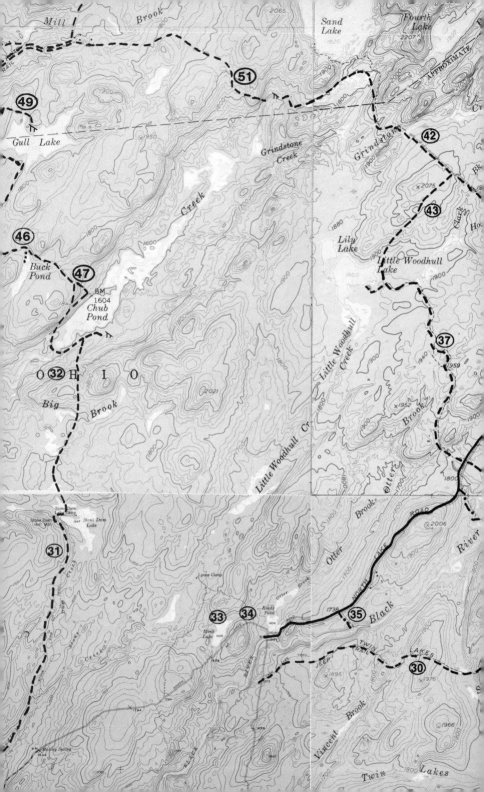

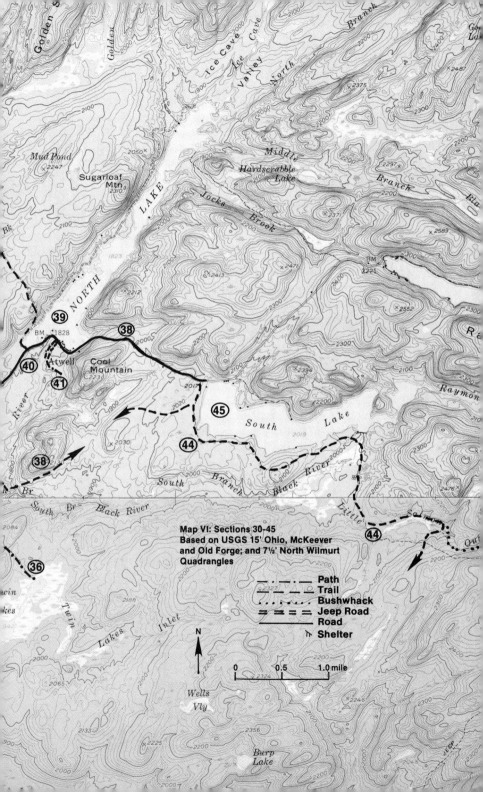

Map VI: Sections 30-45
Based on USGS 15' Ohio, McKeever
and Old Forge; and 7½' North Wilmurt
Quadrangles

Path
Trail
Bushwhack
Jeep Road
Road
Shelter

this section has as much to offer in winter as is available to the hiker in summer. Some of the distances are quite long, however, so plan your outings accordingly.

31 Stone Dam Lake

Trail, hiking, easy grades, hunting, camping
3.5 miles, 1½ hours, 200-foot vertical rise

The well-marked hiking trail to Stone Dam Lake makes a delightful trek through a peaceful hardwood forest. Several intermittent streams are easily crossed, wet areas are few, and as of 1986, the trail was free of blowdowns. Although the ascent is steady, it is so slight as to be hardly noticeable. However, there are innumerable small ups and downs and twists and turns on the route, which winds generally a little east of north to the lake.

The trailhead is located on the north side of North Lake Road at the 6.5-mile point, 0.4 mile past Koenig Brothers' Sawmill. There is a guideboard beside the road and room for a couple of cars to pull off the road. The register is downhill at the beginning of the yellow-marked trail that follows an old roadway. To the left of the register is a narrow footpath, one of several in this area that lead toward Little Woodhull Creek.

The trail reaches high ground above Little Woodhull Creek in 0.25 mile and follows the eastern shore for 0.6 mile, to a bridge, a twenty-minute walk from the trailhead. The tall forest along the creek is rich with hemlock and as handsome as you can find. Throughout this walk, much of the forest cover is open beneath a high canopy, sheltering a rich understory of ferns.

At 0.85 mile, you cross the split-plank bridge with its hand cable. It looks fragile, but it is really substantial. Above the bridge there is a stillwater, under it, a small waterfall, and downstream a lovely series of rapids. You will find a tiny campsite right across the creek.

A fifteen-minute walk past the creek you pass an erratic and you can still hear the creek—you are following the valley of Stone Dam Outlet, but far enough from this tiny stream to be unaware of it. After an hour of walking, you are beside a small rift with rock outcrops. Beyond there is a small but difficult wet area. From here on there is little variation in the scenery, but the distance passes quickly. You walk through an area where large tree trunks lie moss-covered on the forest floor, perhaps the results of a very old blowdown.

Stone Dam Lake

Then the wetlands of Stone Dam Lake appear through the trees to the east. Soon, the main body of water comes into view and you find yourself on a small spruce-lined rise, probably an esker. This is the closest the trail comes to the lake, and it is a good point to depart for explorations. A peninsula extends out from the north shore and it is here, just inside the trees, that the remains of an old lean-to camp are found. A crude table and some benches along with pots, pans, and other hardware indicate that hunters and campers still use the location.

The lake occupies only a fraction of the area originally dammed; shores of the shallow body of water are lined with sundew, leatherleaf, and other bog plants. These meadows extend south along the sinuous outlet as well as to the north of the peninsula.

The trail continues northwest along the esker; there is a small, jet black pool to the left of the trail just before the northern marshes come into view to the right. By continuing up the trail a short distance, you will come to a stream where there is an informal campsite.

32 Chub Pond from Stone Dam Lake

Trail, lean-tos, hiking, fishing, blowdown area
2 miles, 1¼ hour, 150-foot vertical rise

The yellow-marked trail continues north from Stone Dam Lake, through 2 miles of lesser-travelled terrain, to a junction with the blue-marked Chub Pond trail. This route does not follow an old road, or even a traditional hiking route. It has been marked expressly for hikers and because it is so little used, there is only a faint foot tread to follow in places. There are plenty of blue markers to guide the way, but much of the route is through featureless terrain so that if you stray from the trail, it is possible to recross it and never see it. And, unlike most Adirondack trails, here you really need the markers to find the way.

From the inlet stream at the west end of the Stone Dam marshes, you climb a small rise, pass several small marshes, and cross and recross an intermittent stream. After twenty minutes of winding along ridges you reach a dense ferny valley with notably tall maple and beech. You cross a steep knoll, and at 1.2 miles, after a forty-minute walk, reach Big Brook.

The trail, still heading north, ascends to a height-of-land at 1.6 miles, then begins the descent into the Woodhull Creek Valley. Fifteen minutes after you cross Big Brook, you find yourself in a draw with an intermittent stream which the trail crosses and recrosses. Then, suddenly, after just short of an hour's walk, you round a bend in the draw and enter a scene of unbelievable destruction. On August 30, 1984, heavy thunder and lightning storms accompanied by high winds hit the Boonville area. Moving east, they touched down at Chub Pond, levelling an area a half mile or more long and several hundred yards wide. Nothing prepares you for the eerie feeling you get as you enter the devastated landscape. If this was caused by a tornado, the breadth of the pattern of destruction seems much wider than you would expect.

The trail through the blowdown area has been cleared and is well-marked, but walking through giant "jackstraws", upturned root masses, and giant tree tops will remind you of the great forces of nature. Ferns, like the wet forest *Dryopteris clintoniana*, take on strange stunted forms as they find themselves struggling in the dried duff. Brambles and vines are rushing in to cover the area.

The trail winds up and down over newly created knolls, and though the walk through the blowdown area is short—less than 0.2 mile—it will take nearly fifteen minutes to reach a junction with the blue-marked trail that also has red snowmobile trail markers. The yellow trail ends here.

Hurricane Destruction near Chub Pond

If you turn right along the snowmobile trail, which has several wet places, you reach the eastern shore of the pond in a wet grassy meadow with blue flag, bottled gentian, and yellow bladderwort. The shoreline is no place for a picnic. However, the blue trail, which forks right from the snowmobile trail 100 yards north of the intersection, leads into a hollow. It is only a five-minute walk from the intersection down into the hollow, across a footbridge, to one of the best constructed lean-tos in the Adirondacks. At one time, individuals could obtain a permit to build a lean-to on public lands with the understanding that it would be open to all who pass through. Such is the case here, but today it is a most unusual sight to see this well-chinked log structure sitting in the midst of the valley of destruction. Incredibly, none of the blowdown, though close to the lean-to, even touched it.

A left turn at the junction will take you through the center of the blowdown area to the outlet, 0.5 mile away. This portion of trail has some nasty wet spots, but the blowdown is so dense, it is impossible to leave the trail route.

Standing on the wooden bridge over the outlet, you see the widened expanse of Woodhull Creek known as Chub Pond. The trail continues along the northwest edge of the pond, to a second and more scenically located lean-to and the trail north to Bear Creek Road, section 47. This route is shorter than the one outlined, for if you make the trek from North Lake Road, via Stone Dam Lake, and explore the blowdown area, you will walk 13 miles in a minimum of 7 hours.

33 Mink Lake
Path, shrub wetland

Beyond the Koenig Brothers' Sawmill, buildings are few along North Lake Road; the woods grow thicker and the road begins to climb what is known locally as Mulchi Hill. Older folks remember a time when the roads were primitive and the descent of the two steep sections near Mink Lake and Reeds Pond were hazardous for horse-drawn carts or the early automobiles. The pavement of today makes travel much easier, but frost heaves and muddy washes in this area let you know this road is not yet completely tamed.

At the bottom of the first descent, look for Mink Lake through the trees to the left. A small, not-easy-to-spot turnout at 9.4 miles has enough room

Flume on the Black River

for one or two cars to park. From here a path leads down the bank for 100 yards to the brushy shoreline. The vegetation here is typical of the shrub wetlands found throughout the Adirondacks, and many game and song birds reside here. Because it is so difficult to approach the shore, the best way to appreciate the marshes is from a canoe. The carry from the road is short, 150 yards, but good launching spots along the dense shore are hard to find.

34 Reeds Pond
Canoeing, camping, fishing

Ten miles up North Lake Road, after a series of descents, Farr Road, section 29, comes in from the right, south. On the left lies Reeds Pond, the outlet of which flows under the road and plunges into the Black River, 0.1 mile away. In the last half of the nineteenth century, a sawmill operated by the Reed family was located here. Today, the pond is a popular fishing and camping spot. There are large parking areas and room for tents, trailers, and campers on both sides, the westernmost being the most desirable, and the most quickly filled.

It is an easy matter to launch a canoe on the western shore and paddle leisurely north to the pond's major tributary, Otter Brook, which flows in from the north. You can not go far up the brook; after you encounter a few small beaver dams, alders close in and you must turn around. It is, however, a quiet place to be and there is a good chance of seeing beavers, muskrats, and otters.

35 Flume on the Black River
Short path, waterfall, picnic site, swimming, fishing

Drive north from Reeds Pond on a relatively straight stretch of North Lake Road. There is a turnout at 10.8 miles, near a Forest Preserve sign. A well-defined path leads south-southeast from here, crossing private land and passing between some camps. Local people say that the route has long been a traditional way for fishermen to reach the Black River, 0.25 mile away. Respect for the landowners' property is the key to continuing use of this route to the flume. At present, a bushwhack around the property would be the only alternate access.

Twin Lakes Inlet

In the five minutes it takes to walk the path, you cross a small wooden bridge, ascend a knoll to the private land, and, avoiding a side trail leading to a camp on the left, pass quite close to the camp on the right. Beyond the camps, the path drops steeply down the bank to river level. It is easy to lose the path here, but ahead through the trees, you can see the slabs of bedrock where you may picnic and relax after a swim. The river narrows here and shoots through a flume along the left bank. You will want to photograph the beauty of this idyllic spot; its cleanliness and unspoiled character should inspire visitors to maintain its scenic quality.

36 Twin Lakes from the Northwest
Path, large wetland, campsites, hunting, fishing

Twin Lakes has long been accessible from North Lake Road by way of an informal hunter's path. Sporadic axe and paint blazes as well as wet areas and blowdown make the route difficult to follow. The cables that once spanned the Black River are down, and wading across is arduous because of the water's depth. With all this considered, do not be surprised if it takes more than an hour to reach the lakes.

At 11.5 miles, the pavement ends near some camps and North Lake Road climbs to the top of "Railroad Hill." It then begins a steady descent. Though the road receives regular maintenance, this area is sensitive to erosion. Look for a small turnout on the right near a Forest Preserve sign at the 12.8-mile point. The path descends quickly from here to the river.

Across the river, the path heads southeast over a knoll and soon skirts to the left of a wet area. In the next 0.6 mile, you climb in an easterly direction, 250 feet to a saddle, on the way passing the remains of an old camp on the left. This was a makeshift outpost illegally erected on state land and dismantled by the DEC. Only a scattering of hardware remains.

Once past the height-of-land, a gradual descent southeast leads through a difficult wet area and finally terminates near the northern edge of Twin Lakes, section 30. There are several campsites here and all are marred by excessive litter. Fuel cans, bottles, and pieces of plastic spoil this otherwise wild setting.

37 Little Woodhull Lake

Old road, snowmobile trail, fishing, camping, cross-country skiing
3.3 miles, 1½ hours, 150-foot vertical rise

At one time, the North Lake area had a fine system of snowmobile trails extending from Sand Lake Falls on the northwest to South Lake and beyond on the southeast. These trails passed through many scenic areas and were links in a larger network. They are no longer maintained. Some say that the DEC laid out more trails than it could keep up with its limited budget and personnel. One snowmobile enthusiast said that as machines evolved, winding woodland trails were forsaken for more even terrain where higher-performance machines could be appreciated. There is probably truth in both explanations. One side effect of this is the intrusion of snowmobiles in prohibited areas as some seek new routes to replace the old. Hopefully, this is the type of problem the Unit Management Plans will resolve.

Most of the trails were laid out along old roads and can still be followed. Some make very good ski-touring routes, although blowdown and new growth will slowly close them. Several derelict bridges are encountered on these routes, and already many are unusable.

The trail to Little Woodhull Lake is a prime example of this trail transition. Once a great backwoods trail, it now bears the burdens of neglect and time.

A sign on the left side of the road at 13.1 miles marks the trailhead. Park at the turnout 100 feet up the road on the right side where another snowmobile trail heads toward the Black River, section 38.

Starting north with a short ascent past a sign and some posts, the trail follows an old tote road through a mixed woods. The route is fairly obvious, but an occasional old marker is reassuring. A level stretch leads to a stream crossing, then an easy but steady climb begins. Here new growth fills the trail in places. After walking for thirty minutes, you will come to a high point on the trail where an old, round iron casting rests off to the side. From here you look out on a large area of blowdown, undoubtedly caused by the same storm that hit Chub Pond, sections 32 and 47.

The blowdown here has been an aggravation to many who seek the lake and it presented a great puzzle during the research for this guide because no route through it has been marked. As you descend from the knoll, the route enters the blowdown and becomes impossible to trace. Bushwhacking around in the tangle is fatiguing, and you may encounter tagged or paint-blazed routes others have begun. Do not follow these; they will only lead you astray and into rough terrain. The key to finding the trail is on the 1954 USGS topographic map of Old Forge. It accurately shows the course of an old route, most of which became the snowmobile trail. At elevation 1959, the old route divided, only to have its two forks reunite again in 0.25 mile. This split is about 200 feet beyond the top of the knoll. The left fork continues straight ahead into the blowdown, passing the site of an old camp near Otter Brook. Pieces of stoves and other hardware now mark the location, if you can find it. The right fork turns off at a ninety-degree angle and this is the snowmobile trail. Careful searching will reveal the corridor, and without too much difficulty, you will soon leave the chaos behind.

You cross Otter Brook and pick up a few markers as the trail descends to the north. A half hour past the blowdown, you come to a heavily littered campsite at the edge of a wetland. The trail leads out through the marsh grass to a major inlet of Little Woodhull Lake, then turns west. After paralleling the inlet for 0.4 mile, the remains of a wooden bridge lie on the rocks in the water where the trail crosses. In times of high water, getting to the other side is difficult. A herd path continues on along the south bank to an informal campsite near the lake.

Once across the inlet, you soon come to a small stream, beyond which a sign on the right points south and reads "Trail to North Lake Road." This is a junction where a side trail heads west for 0.1 mile to Little Wood-hull Lake. It recrosses the stream and ends at a campsite near the boggy shore. The main trail continues on for 1.5 miles to a trail between North Lake and Sand Lake Falls, sections 42 and 43.

Bushwhacking around Little Woodhull Lake is difficult, but such a beautiful place deserves further exploration. The long, narrow outlet is surrounded by acres of varied wetlands with a sculpture garden of dead standing timber amidst the shrubs and grasses. Large rocks and bleached logs interrupt the swampy shoreline and wildlife abounds. There is a campsite on the north shore, but it is littered and hard to reach. Winter travelers will find the going easier and may wish to go further and explore Lily Lake to the northwest.

38 Between North Lake Road and South Lake

Snowmobile trail, fishing, camping, canoeing
1.6 miles hiking, 5 miles canoeing, 3 hours round trip

A snowmobile trail once ran from North Lake Pond to South Lake crossing the Black River and passing close to its South Branch. Though this section has been abandoned, it is still used by people wishing to canoe or fish. The trail begins from the turnout on the southeast side of the road, 100 feet up from the Little Woodhull Lake trailhead. It is only 0.2 mile to the Black River, but there are no markers and the beginning and two diverging logging roads make the way a bit unclear. Bear right at both intersections and follow the obvious course heading southeast and you will be at the water's edge in less than five minutes. An elaborate wooden bridge, reinforced with cables and supported in the middle by a wooden pier, once allowed safe passage. It now lies in ruin, the near half submerged and pointing downstream, the far half tilted and unstable. Brush, limbs, and a large trunk have snagged on the wreckage. Only by swimming or floating can you reach the far side.

Once across the river, new growth, blowdown, and wet areas make the trail less visible. But old markers, blazes, and a herd path make it possible to follow the route for another 0.6 mile to a campsite near the South

Branch. Markers are now scarce and a good measure of "woodscraft" is required to continue. Eventually nature wins out, and less than a mile from the South Branch, the trail disappears. If you decide to search further, beware of paint blazes and flagging.

It is easy to carry a canoe from the road to the Black River and enjoy an hour or two of paddling. You cannot go far upstream before the way becomes rocky, so head downstream through some quick shallows where it may be necessary to wade or carry for a few yards. The South Branch comes in on the left at 0.4 mile and it is navigable for about 0.3 mile before snags and shallows send you back.

Beyond the South Branch, the river widens. Next you pass the path to Twin Lakes, section 36. The following short, swift section is easily negotiated and the next mile is smooth paddling. Soon, a few large boulders rise out of the water, inviting sandbars appear on the right, and ahead you see many rocks and rapids. This is the end of the navigable flat water, 2.5 miles from the bridge. Just upstream from the sandbars, a long wooden structure lies underwater. Whether it was part of a dam, bridge, or something else, is lost in history.

39 North Lake
Picnicking, camping, canoeing, fishing, swimming

At 14.7 miles, the woods beside North Lake Road open up and the waters of North Lake lie ahead in a fault valley with Ice Cave Mountain looming in the distance. Several camps dot the near shores, but the lands along the upper half are owned by the J. P. Lewis Paper Company.

North Lake is 3.3 miles long and the far end has many bays and inlets. You can easily spend a day exploring, fishing, and watching ducks, loons, kingfishers, and other birds. A road branches off to the left and leads around the state-owned southwest end of the lake to some camps and the J. P. Lewis holdings. There are several areas to park along the state land and many places to fish, picnic, launch a canoe, pitch a tent, or park a camper. This road is not plowed in winter.

Taking the main road straight ahead, you cross the spillway on a steel deck bridge and pass the State House on the right where the gatekeeper lives. Curving right, the road goes along the top of the earthen dam that contains six floodgates. Beyond several private camps, the road crosses a levee and then bears left, paralleling the shore before swinging southeast away from the lake.

40 Atwell Martin's Wigwam Site
Path to local historic site

Atwell Martin, "the hermit of North Lake," came to the area in the mid-1800s after an unhappy love affair led him to despise women. He built a bark shanty (he called it a wigwam) and decorated it with animal bones to ward off witches. Not completely shut off from society, he became the first gatekeeper of the new dam in 1855 and moved into the new structure built for the gatekeeper, which was called the State House. Atwell was uncomfortable in those surroundings, and, following his primitive heart, he moved back into his wigwam. For visitors on North Lake Road, the site has been a curiosity for a century.

To find the site, go down the side road along state land for 0.1 mile and look for a post on the left with a broken snowmobile trail sign. A path leads southwest another 0.1 mile along an old road to a clearing. In the center is a pile of stones and pipes, one of which supports an old metal sign that is shot full of holes. The writing is rapidly fading and two words are illegible. It says, "Here . . . years lived Atwell Martin the North Lake Hermit in his wigwam cabin."

When the settlement of North Lake got its own United States Post Office, it was named Atwell. The Post Office is long gone, but the name Atwell is still used on many maps.

41 Monument Park
Path along an old road to large erratics

Hidden in the woods, just south of North Lake, there are about a dozen large glacial erratics. Known locally as Monument Park, the site was at one time quite an attraction for camp owners and visitors. Byron Cool, turn-of-the-century conservationist, saloon keeper, gatekeeper, and first postmaster of Atwell, once maintained a trail to the area. Today, in the absence of attention and in the wake of natural forces, the regenerated forest has swallowed up the monoliths.

To find them, drive over the spillway, past the State House, and across the earthen dam. At the far end of the dam, just beyond a small camp on the right, a dirt road turns off to the southwest to some camps. Follow this road, bearing left at an intersection at 0.1 mile. After crossing a stream,

Atwell Martin's Wigwam Site

you will come to a small gravel pit on the left where you may park, 0.4 mile from North Lake Road. Just beyond the pit, follow an old logging road, heading left into the woods. In 100 feet, the road splits. Take the right fork branching southeast and pass through a wet area for about 100 yards. As you come to a rise in the road, you will see two large erratics off to the left. Turning south and going downhill, you will see more off to the right. Area residents who frequented the site noticed the individuality of each rock and bestowed such names on them as "Haystack," the "Cabins," and the "Steps."

42 Sand Lake Falls from North Lake
Old road, hiking, cross-country skiing, abandoned snowmobile trail, fishing, swimming, lean-to, waterfall
5.3 miles, 2½ hours, moderate grades

Sand Lake Falls and its lean-to are located along a remote section of Wood-hull Creek, a mile below Sand Lake. A snowmobile trail leading from North Lake to Bear Creek Road and Woodgate passed the lean-to, but the abandonment of the trail now makes the site seem even more isolated. The approach described here is the poorer one for hikers, since it was never maintained as a foot trail. Section 51 describes the route from the west, which also lends itself to a through trip.

Brushy wetlands along the northern half of the trail make walking this route extremely difficult and dry feet are a virtual impossibility. However, locked in the frozen embrace of winter, this may be the preferred route for skiers. The old trail is well-defined, many markers remain visible, blowdowns present few obstacles, moderate hills provide some excitement, and the wetlands invite exploration.

Turn left before the spillway bridge and follow the dirt road around the southwest end of the lake to a point at 0.4 mile where you can see the old trail climbing to the left. This is the steepest part of the whole trip. You gain 150 feet in 0.3 mile. Leveling off, the trail heads generally northwest through a tall hardwood-dominated woods with gentle contours. Take time to search the tops of the mature beech trees for huge "nests." These are made by black bears who climb up to feed on beech nuts and pile the twigs up underneath them. Claw-scarred trunks are further evidence.

As you continue northwest, you cross two small streams, Nelson and Howie creeks. Use care, since the planks or logs thrown across them are usually unreliable and may contain hazardous gaps that snow can hide. After an hour of hiking, you descend about 100 feet to cross a third stream, Clark Brook, and quickly climb again to your former elevation. During this ascent, at a point about 2.5 miles from North Lake Road, a vague junction is reached with a snowmobile trail coming in from the southwest. It leads in 1.5 miles to Little Woodhull Lake, section 37.

After cresting the hill, the trail begins a steady descent to a wetland surrounding Grindstone Creek. A small bridge of questionable durability crosses the creek upstream to the right. Once across, the trail heads west, then north over a few ups and downs, reaching the boundary of the Adirondack League Club at 4 miles. Turning left, you descend and enter the upper reaches of a large wetland where the outlet of the Fourth Bisby Lake meets Woodhull Creek. In times of low water, you can easily wade across the narrow, rocky creek bed above the bridge, but high-water crossings are precarious due to a strong flow.

On the north side of the creek, the trail dips briefly into the woods, then heads southwest along the north edge of the wetland. After another brief detour into the woods, the trail follows the wetland almost to its end. When the trail enters the woods at the west end of the wetland, it is only 0.2 mile further to the lean-to, which faces across a large clearing toward the creek, 100 feet away.

The lean-to is in good condition and the area around it is attractive. There is room for tents nearby; paths behind the lean-to lead to a privy and a large junk pile. The snowmobile trail continues on from the west end of the clearing to a junction with the trail system near Bear Creek, section 51. The continuing route is marked with blue hiking trail markers as well as the orange snowmobile ones.

Sand Lake Falls is not visible from the lean-to. Crossing the clearing, you come to the top of the bedrock slabs that drop to the right, forming the falls. It is not very high and the water does not drop into a free fall, but it has a wild beauty. Pools at the base of the falls and in the rocky stretch beyond afford good swimming and the angling camper will want to try his luck at each one. In the springtime and during wet seasons, the water thunders through here, carrying the combined output of Woodhull, Sand, and the four Bisby lakes.

The 10.6-mile round trip and additional explorations will take the better part of a day.

43 Little Woodhull Lake Link Trail

Abandoned snowmobile trail, hiking, cross-country skiing
1.5 miles, 1 hour, 140-foot vertical rise

From the trail to Sand Lake Falls, section 42, at the point 2.5 miles from North Lake Road, be alert for a widening of the trail and a tree on the right with a cable wrapped around it. This is the junction where a vague path comes in from the left. It gradually descends to the southwest through hardwood forest into the dense mixed-woods basin of Little Woodhull Lake, joining its trail at 1.5 miles, section 37. The route is hard to find in places and markers are not as abundant as they once were, so care and experience are required to stay on the proper course. By combining the three trails, a loop of 8.7 miles is formed which includes also the 1.5 miles of North Lake Road between trailheads.

44 Little Salmon Lake from South Lake Road

Old Road, abandoned snowmobile trail, difficult bushwhack,
hiking, cross-country skiing, fishing, hunting, camping

The state of the old trail to Little Salmon Lake is so bad that this must be considered a bushwhack, and a difficult one at that. The 12-mile round trip takes more than six hours and should be attempted only by those with woods experience.

Past the State House at North Lake, the road is officially designated South Lake Road. After contouring around the south end of the lake, it turns southeast and climbs over a shoulder of Cool Mountain. At 16.7 miles, there is a clearing on the right and an old road leads south from it. For many years, logging operations in the lands to the south brought their loads out over this route. They left behind a confusing network of tote roads, innumerable clearings, and several old camps. Some may find it enjoyable to follow these old roads and explore the clearings. Others may find the unchanging terrain dull. All will agree that it is easy to lose your sense of direction and distance in such a maze. Use your compass faithfully and note landmarks at intersections. The clearings make good campsites.

Little Salmon Lake lies southeast of South Lake, section 45, and was at one time easily reached by following the right combination of logging roads. Later, a snowmobile trail was laid out and maintained over several of these roads. It paralleled South Lake's western and southern shores and went west and south of Little Salmon Lake to connect with the old Herkimer Road which it followed to Nobleboro, section 25. Much of this wide, grassy trail is still used by snowmobiles and all-terrrain vehicles, but it does not appear to have been officially maintained for years and the markers are slowly disappearing. It makes a very good cross-country skiing trail and it is the route you will follow most of the way.

Park at the clearing and proceed straight into the woods on the old trail. A dirt road branches off immediately to the left and leads past a small campsite on the right to a second, larger campsite on the western edge of South Lake. The rocky shore is also a nice spot for picnicking and swimming.

Five minutes down the trail, an old road comes in from the right. This is the other end of the snowmobile trail from North Lake Road, section 38. It leads west, passing through a flooded area and into a maze of lumber roads. Markers are rare at the beginning and absent after twenty-five minutes, making it virtually impossible to determine the correct route. Use care if you choose to explore this area.

The main trail (though with the markings disappearing, this guide should technically call it a path) continues south through a few nasty mudholes and over an occasional patch of old corduroy. Turning east, you begin a slight ascent. The way is drier and walking becomes more pleasant. After walking for twenty-five minutes, you will see a side trail heading left to three camps on the south shore. The trail soon levels off, descends slightly, then ascends another hill. In the descent that follows, a faint path enters on the left. It leads to an old camp built up on piers on the south shore.

Next you come to a split in the trail where an old road branches left, only to rejoin your route in a few minutes. Bear right, and in five minutes the trail crosses a second outlet of South Lake, created when the rising waters of the new reservoir found a low spot here. You will see a two-foot concrete dam to the left with the lake beyond. The bridge here is just a pile of rotting logs and is awkward to walk. As you climb beyond this, you pass a small, swampy area on the left and come to an intersection where an old road heads left to the top of the dam, 0.1 mile away. Past this intersection, the trail descends to a grassy clearing where another old road goes left for an extremely wet 0.1 mile to the gatehouse at the foot of the dam and a small campsite. It will take you a little over an hour to reach this clearing, 2.7 miles from South Lake Road.

The path now widens and crosses the South Branch of the Black River on a decaying log bridge; then the path swings south. A ten-minute walk past the bridge, you cross a small stream and enter a clearing where a lumber camp once stood. There were at least six buildings and sheds here; the ruins of one can be seen to the right. At a fork in the trail ahead, bear left; the right fork leads to a network of logging roads. In the next 1.5 miles, the trail ascends, swings east, contouring around a hill, and passes three small clearings. Bear right at each clearing, and forty-five minutes from the South Lake dam you cross a stream on logs. A minute later, you cross the outlet of Little Salmon Lake on logs and enter a large clearing on the far side. The ruins of an old lumber camp are found at this spot where several old, grown-in roads converge. The snowmobile trail turns right here and heads southwest becoming lost in a jumble of logging roads. It is unclear which way the trail went to connect up with the old Herkimer Road since the markers have disappeared. If you decide to explore this dense, remote area, *use extreme caution*. Keep track of landmarks and directions and do not travel alone. There is a local claim that ore in the area can cause a compass to give erroneous readings. Backwoods skills and clear thinking are essential.

The sure way to reach Little Salmon Lake is by bushwhacking up its outlet. Start back at the clearing behind the collapsed camp and follow up along the south bank. It is just under 1 mile to the lake, but the woods are dense and there are several areas of beaver flooding. The experienced bushwhacker may be able to follow the faint trace of an old road that paralleled the outlet, higher up and to the south of it, but it is rapidly vanishing. When you eventually reach the lake, you will find its densely-wooded shore makes walking along it difficult.

45 South Lake

Fishing, canoeing, camping, swimming, picnicking

A tall earthen dam, 350 feet long, creates South Lake, filling a large basin near the headwaters of the Black River's South Branch. As at North Lake, there are several camps, most in a cluster near the road and the remaining few along the south shore. However, more than ninety percent of the shoreline is state-owned and densely wooded, making it difficult to find a campsite. Several beaver lodges can be found, and loons and kingfishers are sure to be seen.

At 16.8 miles, just past the clearing and the Little Salmon Lake Trailhead, section 44, a dirt road leads 0.1 mile to a campsite and a picnic spot on the rocky western shore. Beyond here, South Lake Road travels over a short causeway with a swampy area on the left, to a parcel of state land with a parking area and a boat launch at 17 miles. The road, now called Honnedaga Lake Road leads, logically, to that lake, which is owned by the Adirondack League Club. The public can only drive on another 1.8 miles before a steel gate at the Club's boundary turns nonmembers back.

From a small dock at the parking area, launch your canoe and head east, past the camps. Paddling along the north shore you will see two clearings on state land where camps once stood. Halfway down the lake, a campsite sits atop a rocky bluff facing southeast. The land rises steeply from the east shore and the water is deep. If you head south toward the dam, you will see a wide channel entering from the east. A rocky point on the north bank has a tiny campsite probably too close to water to make it legal.

Continue on to the wild east bay. Here notice slabs of bedrock underwater near the narrow entrance. This was probably a waterfall before the reservoir was created. Raymond Brook enters the bay from the east and it is navigable for about 0.5 mile before shallows turn you around.

Another, larger campsite can be found halfway through the channel along the south bank. It is on the east side of a small indentation near a large pyramid-shaped rock in the woods. The south shore has a few little bays worth exploring, and you may wish to stop and walk along the grassy top of the dam. There are many ferns at the west and a faint path leading back to the site of an old building. Two roads lead 0.1 mile to the Little Salmon Lake snowmobile trail, section 44.

From Woodhull Creek to the Moose River

THE WOODHULL CREEK tributary of the Black River was also dammed to provide water for the Black River and Erie canals. Of dams at Chub, Sand, and Woodhull lakes, only the one at Woodhull remains. This dam, completed in 1860, added 800 million cubic feet of storage to the system. To build the dam, a good road was constructed from Woodgate. The earliest account of a trip to Woodhull Lake is of a fishing party of ten that included three women. The group made their way on horseback and by foot from the White Lake Hotel to Woodhull and Sand lakes, where they caught a number of trout and suckers. Throughout the 1860s, this road enabled horse carts to reach such remote places as the Bisby Ponds and even North Lake. Today, Woodhull Road leads to the trips described in sections 46 through 52.

Just south of the Adirondack Park boundary on NY 28 is the hamlet of Woodgate. Here, turn east at an intersection with a flashing light, and follow Bear Creek Road 3.2 miles to its end at a parking area on the Herkimer County line and the Park boundary. This is the beginning of the old Woodhull Road, which led in 6 miles to Woodhull Lake.

Just east of Woodgate, Bear Creek Road crosses the roadbed of the Adirondack Railroad. You will cross it as you head to trails east of McKeever, Thendara, and Forestport Station. Much has been written about the construction of this railroad, which opened up the wild western Adirondacks. Now its future is in limbo even though private concerns periodically express an interest in its revitalization. There are numerous proposals to tear up the tracks and maintain the route for hiking and snowmobiling, uses for which it now unofficially serves. While some sections are in disrepair and others are long and monotonous, it is a viable hiking right-of-way, providing access to remote areas that delight history students and railroad buffs.

The region's second major trailhead is near McKeever, which lies to the east of NY 28 on the south side of the Moose River. The road leads past a few camps then curves to the left. Bear right at this curve, passing in front of the old railroad station, which is now a private residence. This road crosses the tracks and leads to a large parking area 0.7 mile from the

Map VII: Sections 46-61
Based on USGS 15' McKeever
and Old Forge Quadrangles

0   0.5   1.0 mile

N

Path
Trail
Bushwhack
Jeep Road
Proposed location of Panther Dam

Shelter

highway. To the left of a register and a large signboard map is the beginning of a snowmobile trail that follows an old jeep trail east to Woodhull Lake. This trail is much abused by vehicular use and is not desirable for hiking or skiing. Therefore it is not described in this guide.

Paralleling the snowmobile trail to the north, a fire truck trail follows the course of an old railroad grade, east toward Woodhull Mountain. This spur of the Adirondack Railroad was used to haul out timber and was in operation around 1910. Today it is a wide, even corridor, marked as a hiking trail but used by the DEC for vehicular access for administrative purposes. It gives access to destinations described in sections 55 through 61. There is a second parking area 0.1 mile east along this road at the point the road is barred to public vehicular traffic.

In addition to the red, yellow, or blue hiking trail markers, all trails will also have snowmobile trail markers unless otherwise noted in the text.

46 Buck Pond

Snowmobile trail, hiking, cross-country skiing
2.7 miles, 1¼ hours, relatively level

From the Bear Creek Trailhead, follow Woodhull Road with its blue markers northeast for five minutes to a junction. The road continues on ahead with yellow markers to destinations outlined later in this chapter. Turn right onto an old road with a yellow gate. The blue trail follows this road southeast to Buck Pond and on to Chub Pond, section 47.

The trail bends right in an open field and crosses a very small creek through an open marsh on a large bridge, one that can support jeep travel. This may account for the wallows in the road further along. A narrower section of trail follows, then at 1.4 miles there is a wooden bridge over Gull Lake Outlet with lovely open marshes along the creek here.

At 2 miles, there is a junction where a yellow-marked trail heading left leads in 2.1 miles to a trail in the Gull Lake area, section 49. Continuing straight through, the blue-marked trail crosses a stream, then passes a wet area on the right.

About 0.7 mile past this last junction, after one and a quarter hours of walking, you should notice a bog through the trees to the south. Buck Pond lies at the far end of the bog. Many clumps of pitcher plants grow here and though it is not easy walking through the bog, it is worth risking a wet foot to view the lovely specimens of this carnivorous plant. If you walk to the edge of the pond, you can feel the bog quiver beneath your feet. Layers of dense peat and sphagnum mosses float on the water all around this pond in mats so thick they support shrubs and small trees, and, hopefully, curious explorers.

47 Chub Pond

Snowmobile trail, hiking, cross-country skiing, lean-tos, swimming, fishing, blowdown area
3.7 miles, 1¾ hours, 200-foot vertical rise

The blue-marked trail continues on past Buck Pond, section 46, through a small wet area, then begins to descend into the Woodhull Creek Valley to Chub Pond. Near the beginning of the descent, the trail splits. The right fork drops steeply down the hillside to the water's edge and intersects the trail between the lean-tos.

The left fork is a direct route to the state lean-to on the north shore. It is designated "lean-to #2" on trail signs and is the more scenically located of the two. Sitting on a sandy bank overlooking the pond, it is a favorite destination of fishing and camping parties arriving by float plane. There is a picnic table here and the pebbly beach affords good swimming. You may find a rowboat nearby, but its pond-worthiness is questionable. However, if you have the means to do so, explore the wetlands along the northeast extension of the pond. You can boat for a long way through quiet marshes watching marsh harriers glide low over the waving grasses. The place creates a deep sense of remoteness.

From lean-to #2, the blue-marked trail heads southwest, passing both forks and leading through a lush, fern-covered woods along the northwest shore. Many boulders are scattered through this area and ducks frequently take off from hiding places along the bank. You begin to notice the severe blowdown from a storm on August 30, 1984. See section 32 for more details. The magnitude of the destruction increases as you approach the outlet. Crossing the wooden bridge over the outlet, 0.8 mile southwest of the lean-to, the trail passes through the center of the devastated area.

At a junction 0.5 mile from the outlet, a yellow-marked trail heads south to Stone Dam Lake and North Lake Road, sections 31 and 32. The blue marked trail ends at the Plumbly lean-to, less than five minutes beyond the junction. Lean-to #1 (Plumbly) is 5 miles and two and a quarter hours from the Bear Creek Trailhead.

48 Bear Creek

Trail, path, canoeing, fishing, hunting, campsites
1 mile, ½ hour, relatively level

A second junction is reached 0.2 mile past the fork to Chub Pond, along Woodhull Road, about 0.6 mile from the Bear Creek Trailhead. The yellow-marked trail forks left onto an old road with a yellow gate. The Woodhull Road bears right and leads to some private inholdings with camps. Vehicles are allowed to use the 3.3 miles of road from the trailhead to the camps, but beyond this junction, Woodhull Road has deteriorated into a muddy, rutted stretch that is a sad insult to the wild forest surrounding it. Apparently, some of the vehicle operators are unhappy with this situation, for it appears that they frequently use the trail to the north as a bypass. This is a matter that needs to be addressed soon, before a similar eyesore occurs on the hiking trail.

Past the gate, the left fork begins a gradual descent through some fragrant balsams in a small clearing on the right. Next, a sandy clearing is reached and here a path heads left along an old road for 0.1 mile to Bear Creek. This spot is just over a mile from the parking area and there is room to camp here. Old wooden abutments indicate that a bridge once spanned the creek here and old logging roads can be found on the opposite side.

Five minutes further on the yellow-marked trail, after crossing a stream, you reach another sandy clearing. The trail swings right and a second old road forks left, passes a small campsite, and reaches Bear Creek in 200 yards.

Both approaches to the creek are used by fishermen and hunters who recognize the area's abundant wildlife. Large open wetlands upstream provide habitat for great blue herons, ducks, and a variety of song birds. Many deer graze the area and you will see signs of beaver and muskrat.

Canoeing Bear Creek is difficult, due to beaver dams, thickets, and snags, but if you are willing to carry a canoe over a mile to these access points, you will be rewarded by the opportunity to canoe over 2 miles along the twisting course of Bear Creek into these seldom-visited lands.

49 Gull Lake

Hiking, cross-country skiing, lean-to, swimming, fishing
3.6 miles, 1¾ hours, relatively level

The yellow-marked trail that leads to Bear Creek continues northwest paralleling the creek with minor ups and downs. It intersects a red-marked trail at 2.2 miles, about an hour's walk, from the trailhead. This trail, 0.9 mile in length, ascends to the southeast, crossing the muddy Woodhull Road in 0.3 mile.

After gaining 200 feet in elevation, it levels off and ends at a junction with a yellow-marked trail. The sign to the left says the lean-to is 0.5 mile away. You will find it takes about twenty minutes to wind around the northern bays and marshes of the lake, descending over a series of ups and downs to a lean-to nestled in the trees on the north shore of Gull Lake. The lean-to is in good shape and a path leads to the water's edge. If you continue beyond the lean-to 100 yards, there are some handsome rocks for a picnic. Many of the small balsams beyond the lean-to have been cut off. In the old days, balsam boughs were cut to make a soft, fragrant bedding for weary campers, but cutting live wood in the Forest Preserve is illegal.

Back at the junction, continue straight ahead on the yellow trail, southwest along the shore of the lake, where you may find a rowboat chained to a tree. Vehicles occasionally drive from Woodhull Road to this point and the rowboat's owner uses it to get to a private camp, hidden from view at the far end of the lake.

The trail continues back from the lake, where there are nice rock ledges along the shore. Then it heads into a small, dense woods through an evergreen-shaded cut to a bridge over the outlet of Gull Lake. The trail swings to the east now and 1 mile past the junction it passes by a handsome marshy extension of the lake. Dead standing trees and a beaver lodge create a solemn, wild scene.

The trail turns sharply right and follows a southwest course for another 1.1 miles to its junction with the blue-marked trail to Buck and Chub ponds, sections 46 and 47.

50 Bear Lake
Marked trail, hiking, swimming, camping, fishing
5.5 miles, 2½ hours, relatively level

Bear Lake has a charm of its own, as many of its visitors will tell you. Steep hills on the west, north, and east cradle the quiet waters that empty to the south, creating Bear Creek. Depending on beaver flooding, the upper half of this hourglass-shaped lake has sandy beaches that are ideal for swimming, sunbathing, and picnicking. Toward the outlet, the shores become

South Bay of Gull Lake

brushy and the waters are filled with pickerel-weed and water lilies. Tiny sundews can be found clinging to saturated wood lying along the shore. Many types of birds can be observed here, and the variety of animal tracks attests to the lake's popularity as a watering hole.

Even the three trails to Bear Lake offer a pleasant diversion. They are maintained only as foot trails and are a welcome change in an area groomed mostly for motorized travel. The approach from the south described here has the longest stretch of foot trail. At a point 2.5 miles from the Bear Creek Road Trailhead, the yellow-marked trail comes to a junction and curves right. Taking the blue-marked trail on the left, you head north, passing a campsite on the left, and then drop to cross Mill Brook. The trail narrows and parallels Bear Creek, which is out of sight to the west. Easy ups and downs take you across another stream and on to Bear Lake after an hour and a half. On the eastern edge of the lake, a yellow-marked trail comes in from Woodhull Lake, section 59. The blue-marked trail crosses an inlet and continues on around the north shore where it crosses a second inlet, then turns north and heads toward McKeever, section 57. Several campsites can be found along the trail near the lake.

51 Sand Lake Falls

Trail, hiking, swimming, fishing, lean-to, campsites, waterfall
6.1 miles, 3+ hours, 250-foot vertical rise

This is the preferred route for hikers since it is much drier than the route described in section 42. However, as of 1986, there has been no maintenance for many years on the last 2.7 miles of trail, which is now overgrown with only a faint herd path in places. Markers are slowly disappearing, and detouring around blowdowns increases your chances of losing the trail. Good navigational skills are required to follow this route.

Stay on the yellow-marked trail, bearing right at the Bear Lake Trail junction, section 50. In five minutes, the trail rejoins the muddy Woodhull Road and you turn left, heading east. After crossing a stream, the road begins an easy ascent and its condition improves. A brief level stretch is followed by a short descent to a muddy junction where the yellow markers end, 3.4 miles from the Bear Creek Road Trailhead. About 100 yards ahead, you can see one of the several private camps where Woodhull Road curves north to continue on to Woodhull Lake with blue markers, section 52. To your right, the blue-marked Sand Lake Falls Trail heads east through a draw. The first 0.2 mile is poorly defined and very wet until you cross

a stream on a deteriorated wooden bridge. New growth soon fills the trail and you must take your time to follow the old path as it trends a little north of east.

Thirty minutes and 1 mile later, you enter a large, grassy clearing. Legend has it that this was an old homestead where a family once hunted and farmed, and one version of the tale says that they starved during a severe winter. Some claim that they met a grisly fate at the hands of vengeful Indians. Yet another story describes a turn-of-the-century hermitage. All evidence, however, indicates that this was where a lumber camp once stood, and with a little exploration, the site will yield its share of bottles, saw blades, barrel hoops, and horseshoes. While not as sensational a legacy as some would have it, such lumber camps were, in their own way, a colorful part of Adirondack history.

The trail follows along the right edge of the clearing, reenters the woods at its southeast corner, then crosses a stream. Heading east-southeast, you pass through a wet area and begin a gradual ascent where the trail becomes extremely hard to find. Blowdown, dense growth, and scarce markers make the going difficult, especially for those carrying full packs. Finally, a tiring half hour after leaving the clearing, you reach the height-of-land and begin to descend into the Woodhull Creek valley. You may be able to hear the falls from here and give your spirits a lift. Moderate descents lead south, then east-southeast, crossing a few streams. After a brief level section, the trail drops and enters the large clearing with the lean-to on the left and the falls on the right.

52 Woodhull Lake

Trail, hiking, cross-country skiing, lean-to, fishing, swimming
6.8 miles, 3⅓ hours, 300-foot vertical rise

You could say that walking along any part of the Woodhull Road from the trailhead to the area of the private camps near the Sand Lake Falls Trail junction is a 3-D experience: dismal, depressing, and deplorable. Beyond the camps, however, you are in for a pleasant change of scene. For most of its remaining length it is a firm, smooth route and a satisfying, though long approach to Woodhull Lake. It seems especially well suited for ski-touring with enough modest grades and variations in scenery to remain interesting.

Another surprise awaits you as you arrive at the lean-to. It is one of the largest in the Park and can easily accommodate a dozen campers with all their gear. A double fireplace seems to anticipate the appetites of a large group. At one time, this theme was also reflected by the amount of litter present, but much of it has been removed and we should all make certain that the effort continues.

Local tradition and some trail signs refer to the lake as "Big" Woodhull Lake, thus differentiating it from Little Woodhull Lake to the south, sections 37 and 43. The 1958 McKeever and the 1954 Old Forge USGS topographic maps label it Woodhull Lake, which maintains continuity with the names of the mountain and the creek.

Passing to the left of the camps beyond the Sand Lake Falls Trail junction, section 51, the blue-marked Woodhull Road drops to cross Mill Brook. Heading generally northeast, you next begin a long, moderately easy ascent, broken by a few short, level stretches. The route is just east of north for 1 mile, then north of east for 1.5 miles. After an hour, you reach the height-of-land as well as a few wet areas. The road grade is dramatically evident here as ditches on both sides follow for a ways. A brief descent takes you to a small open area where the trail turns sharply to the left. At this point, the unmarked Woodhull Road continues straight ahead, up over a hill and down to Woodhull Lake, 0.7 mile away. It can be easily followed for about 0.5 mile to the boundary of the Adirondack League Club, where it fades.

The blue-marked trail heads north through a swamp for about 150 yards. A herd path has formed along the right edge of the swamp making the hike somewhat easier, but you must cross part of the wet area to get to a wooden bridge over an inlet. Leaving the swamp, the trail passes over rolling terrain for nearly a mile, the space of a twenty-minute walk, then descends to a junction. Ahead, the blue-marked trail crosses a bridge and leads to the McKeever Truck Trail, section 58. A muddy trail comes in from the right and it leads 300 yards to the lean-to. The rocky shore and sandy bottom are just right for swimming, and the view across the lake is peaceful—good rewards for the long hike in.

53 Granny Marsh
Path, bushwhack, hunting
2.5 miles, 1½ hours, relatively level

Adirondack wetlands are the oases of the north woods. Most woodland creatures depend on wetlands in a variety of ways at one time or another in their lives. The open water is a place for amphibians to breed, fish to grow, insects to develop during their aquatic stages, and migratory waterfowl to land. Grasses along the edges support a variety of birds with cover and nesting places and supply muskrat colonies with needed food and building material. Aquatic plants are staples in the diets of the transient moose populations and the white-tailed deer, who each winter "yard up" in the open fields surrounded by protective stands of dense conifers. This diversity of wildlife also calls the predator and raptor who sustain themselves on the old and the weak.

Granny Marsh, lying southeast of Otter Lake, is typical of Adirondack wetlands. The nature observer is sure to appreciate the varied vegetation and the signs of several different animals. It is best visited in the winter when snow and ice permit easier travel and offer protection to the surrounding plant life. The woods between it and Otter Lake are mostly open hardwoods and any bushwhack route with the proper compass bearing will get you there. The description given here offers a varied approach with a little history added.

An old snowmobile trail heads east into the woods 0.7 mile south of the flashing lights in the village of Otter Lake, across from the Chute Inn tavern. Parking may be possible if you ask permission at any one of the local establishments. Using the snowmobile trail as a point of entry, head east and intercept the railroad tracks. Your immediate objective is to reach Purgatory Creek, so turn south and follow the tracks for 0.5 mile to a culvert through which the creek flows west. An alternate approach, instead of following the tracks, is to cross them and continue east to a long clearing. This was once a grass airstrip. By heading southeast from its south end, you will soon pick up Purgatory Creek. Follow this pretty little creek upstream along its north bank, crossing a small tributary in half an hour.

By now you will see a faint path along the north bank. It begins at a driveway up behind the old Otter Lake General Store and follows an old pipeline coming from a small reservoir on Purgatory Creek that you will reach in another five minutes. A small, overgrown concrete and stone dam creates a pond that once supplied water to a hotel near the train station.

The path continues around to the left of the pond and crosses an inlet. Heading now in a magnetic south direction, it becomes obscure in a dense, wet area. If you manage to stay with it, you will come to a hunting camp at the edge of the state land boundary in half an hour. However, to reach Granny Marsh, leave the path beyond the pond and follow a bearing of 126° magnetic southeast. This will take you through a mile of mature hardwoods to a ridge northwest of the wetland, which should be visible through the trees. Avoid descending to the north, where dense evergreen thickets make travel difficult. Once down in the open, you will want to explore the inlets at each end. You may even want to bushwhack southeast over a ridge to the wetlands along Bear Creek. A full day can be spent studying this wild, peaceful area.

54 Brewer Lake

Snowmobile trail, old road, fishing, swimming, camping, path
1.9 miles, 1 hour, 300-foot vertical rise

It was once decided that pretty Brewer Lake, with its natural rock dam, would support a hatchery for trout, so the lake was poisoned and stocked. It has been popular with fishermen ever since and there used to be three boats in the area. One is near the eastern shore, but it has been used as a target and lost its water-worthiness. If other boats still exist, they are hidden.

The trail begins at the former Otter Lake General Store on the east side of NY 28, just south of the flashing lights. From the store parking lot, cross the railroad tracks on a driveway that abruptly turns left. It leads to a snowmobile trail with a barred gate before curving right and going to some camps. Hike northeast on the snowmobile trail, a smooth, grassy, old woods road that has very few markers. After twenty minutes, a path comes in from the left; avoid it on your return.

The trail slowly gains elevation and begins a wide swing east, then south. Steepness increases, the woods become more dense and some blowdown lies across the trail. You cross a wet area; on the left lies an old section of wooden culvert. It is doubtful that snowmobiles go much further beyond here. The trail narrows, patches of bedrock appear, and the top of the ridge is reached. As you start to descend, the trail becomes muddy and overgrown in places, making navigation difficult. As the trail swings to the east, it becomes easier to follow and you quickly come to the western edge of the lake. A path goes around most of the lake. It seems to be routinely brushed out and leads to several informal campsites. The nicest one is on the eastern edge by a large boulder. The rocky shoreline is the best place for swimming. Unfortunately, the signs of over-use are all too evident here.

For the truly adventurous, there is a more direct route following an old path. A highly resourceful, if not altogether ecologically minded individual marked this path using red paint, tape, reflectors, can and bottle covers, taillight lenses and vintage hubcaps. Blowdown and negligence, however, make the path quite difficult to follow.

As you walk the driveway described in the beginning of this section, pass by the snowmobile trail and swing right, heading up toward the camps. You will see the path coming in from the left. Heading generally west, it climbs into a section of tall black cherry trees, then dips into a wet area. After crossing a stream, you begin to climb and an interesting rock outcrop appears on the right. At the top of the outcrop, the path swings right and levels out. Perhaps the supply of markers ran out here, for the path fades away. It is wise to head toward magnetic east for the remaining 0.3 mile to the lake. The total distance is about 1.5 miles.

55 Brewer Lake from the North
Bushwhack

For the bushwhacker, this route provides a much more interesting approach to Brewer Lake than the trail described in section 54. It takes about one and a half hours to cover the 2.5-mile one-way hike with its 300-foot climb.

From the McKeever Trailhead (see introduction to this chapter for directions) follow the red-marked truck trail 0.1 mile to a second register. It is possible to drive here and park along the side. A yellow gate prevents further travel, but snowmobiles and ATVs sometimes violate this barrier. Markers are scarce, but the way is obvious and after a twenty-minute walk you cross a stream coming in from the southwest. Leave the trail and head up along this stream as it tumbles over bedrock from one small pool to another. You pass a rock outcrop on the right and soon come to the snowmobile trail that runs from the parking lot to Woodhull Lake. It is clear that more than snowmobiles use that trail since the deep ruts and mudholes are the work of four-wheel-drive vehicles. Before the State Land Master Plan went into effect, this old road was considered a traditional jeep road. Unfortunately, this tradition continues in what seems to be a violation of the law. Even though a Wild Forest designation makes allowances for motorized access, it is supposed to be limited to snowmobile travel on designated trails or other motorized travel on vehicular rights-of-way to private inholdings. Some may argue whether the situation here violates the law, but that it violates the environment is indisputable.

Not far beyond the snowmobile trail, a long, open area is reached. Proceed along its western edge and notice the relatively new beaver pond with the lodge built, oddly enough, in the middle of the dam. Quiet, patient

Woodhull Lake

observation may be rewarded by the appearance of one of these master builders. At the upper end of the pond, an ancient beaver dam lies in ruin; the grassy meadow behind it indicates that area that was once flooded.

As the meadow narrows, it swings to the southeast. You should leave the area at this curve and follow a bearing of 217° magnetic. The land will begin to rise through an open hardwood forest and you will find yourself ascending a ridge with a few interesting erratics along your line of travel. Near the top of the ridge, about twenty-five minutes past the beaver meadow, head magnetic south and in five minutes you should see the water of Brewer Lake through the trees. The descent from the ridge top is steep and you have to cross many striking rock outcrops as you negotiate the 100-foot descent. The northwest shore of the lake is quickly reached and a campsite is not far away along the path described in section 54.

56 Squirrel Ponds
Bushwhack

What man has done to the lower Black and Raquette rivers, beavers have done in miniature to a tiny stream in a deep ravine west of Bear Lake.

Though the beavers are currently inactive, the chain of ponds remains behind several small dams, at least seven in half a mile. You can bushwhack to these ponds on a 2.5-mile route that takes one and a third hours and climbs but 250 feet.

Your bushwhack to the Squirrel Ponds begins along the route to Brewer Lake, section 55. When you reach the newer beaver dam beyond the snowmobile trail, follow herd paths along the eastern edge of the pond and meadow. The upper end of the meadow curves south, then east. The land rises and a stream is reached. Head east, following this stream up through a scenic ravine with high rock outcrops. At the head of the ravine, continue through a draw leading south-southeast to an area of dead standing timber at the edge of the uppermost pond. From here, herd paths follow along the banks of the ponds, descending southeast, then turning southwest. The grade lessens after half a mile and the lowest ponds rest in a swampy depression where dense growth makes exploration difficult.

57 Bear Lake from the North

Trail, hiking, swimming, fishing, picnicking, camping
2.5 miles, 1¼ hours, 300-foot vertical rise, 250-foot descent

This is by far the best route to Bear Lake. It is the shortest and most scenic, and, therefore, the most popular approach.

Walk east along the red-marked truck trail east from the McKeever Trailhead. This hiker's highway is easy with good footing; the woods are parklike and open with a ferny understory. In just under a mile, you cross a stream; and at 1.2 miles, a twenty-minute walk, you reach the marked intersection with a blue-marked trail that heads right, south.

The blue trail begins a long, gradual ascent that closely follows a stream for most of its length. After crossing the rutted snowmobile trail, there is a wet section, then the trail becomes steeper. It angles east through a draw and reaches a height-of-land about forty minutes' walk from the truck trail. Dropping steeply, the trail goes through impressive rock outcrops where several intermittent rivulets emerge to form a sizeable inlet. After reaching the north shore, the trail turns sharply to the left, crosses the inlet, and heads out along the east edge of the lake. Crossing a second inlet, it reaches a junction with the yellow-marked foot trail coming from Bloodsucker Pond and Woodhull Lake to the east, section 59. The blue marked trail continues south to the Woodhull Road and Bear Creek, section 50.

58 Woodhull Lake from the North

Trail, hiking, cross-country skiing, swimming, fishing, lean-to
5 miles, 2¼ hours, 400-foot vertical rise

The red-marked McKeever Truck Trail continues on past the Bear Lake Trail junction with very slight grades, passing two small clearings on the right that are full of bottled gentian in late August. Wetlands lie beside the roadway, which is raised to keep it level. The canopy is closed, making this a cool road to walk even on the warmest day. A thirty-minute walk past the Bear Creek intersection, there is on the left a large meadow full of raspberries and blackberries and an intriguing old foundation. Five minutes beyond, at 3.1 miles on the truck trail, you reach a four-way intersection. The trail left goes to Remsen Falls, section 61. The trail straight ahead stays on the truck trail and leads to Woodhull Mountain, section 60.

Turn right for Woodhull Lake, crossing a gate and ascending a blue-marked trail heading south to a junction in 0.2 miles. The muddy snowmobile trail from McKeever enters ahead from the right. The blue-marked trail turns sharply left and joins it, descending slightly as it swings south-southeast. Fortunately, the trail is not as eroded here as it is closer to its beginning, and it is tolerable for the remainder of the way to the lake.

In the next 1.5 miles you will gain more than 300 feet of elevation over a series of moderate grades. You cross a few intermittent streams and within an hour reach a height-of-land. An old road branches off to the left and drops in less than 0.2 mile to a clearing on the shore of Woodhull Lake known as Wolf Lake Landing. The trail continues on through the woods, gradually descending to a junction with a link trail that heads west, passing Bloodsucker Pond on its way to Bear Lake, section 59. Just past this junction, a bridge over the Bloodsucker Pond Outlet is crossed, and just beyond the bridge, the muddy trail to the lean-to forks left. The blue-marked trail leads on to the Woodhull Road, section 52, and Bear Creek Road.

Skiers may wish to run the downhill from the height-of-land to Wolf Lake Landing and then traverse the frozen lake surface to the lean-to a little over 0.1 mile down the shore. This way is about 0.2 mile shorter than by trail.

59 Bloodsucker Pond Link Trail

Trail, hiking
1.7 miles, 50 minutes, 250-foot vertical rise, west to east

The eastern end of the Link Trail is quite close to Woodhull Lake. The link is a yellow-marked foot trail that leaves the blue-marked trail just north of the bridge over the Bloodsucker Pond outlet, 1.8 miles south of the four-way junction on the McKeever Truck Trail. Its location makes several loop hikes and side trips possible.

An easy ascent brings you near the edge of Bloodsucker Pond, a small, boggy pond with an old beaver dam at its outlet. Beyond, the trail ascends north for 200 yards, then swings west, beginning a long, gradual descent over rolling terrain to Bear Lake. At 1.3 miles, the trail reaches an attractive stream that flows from the northeast. The trail follows it to the lake where the yellow markers end at a junction with the blue-marked trail, sections 50 and 57.

60 Woodhull Mountain

Trail, hiking, cross-country skiing, snowshoeing, fire tower
7.3 miles, 4 hours, 800-foot vertical rise

This is one of the longest approaches to a fire tower in the Adirondack Park, even though the distance calculated is shorter than that given in the DEC's booklets. Even if the trip could be made under ideal circumstances, it is unsettling to know that on the opposite side of the mountain, a trail 0.7 mile long climbs from the Bisby Road to the summit. But since it is on Adirondack League Club property, the public must use this long western route. The tower has not been manned in recent years and is slated for removal.

The first 5 miles of trail are along the McKeever Truck Trail and you can make good time along it—fifteen minutes to a mile unless you are carrying a pack. Go straight through the four-way junction 2.8 miles from the McKeever Trailhead. Beyond the junction, the truck trail changes little. In ten minutes, you see a lumber clearing and a pond visible through the trees to the left. Many implements and bits of hardware from logging days can be seen here, and some spots are suitable for camping. An earthen levee forms the north bank of the pond, indicating man's development of this former wetland. The levee has been breached in two places, but an active beaver colony has patched it up and now thrives in this former haunt for lumberjacks.

For the next 2 miles, the trail passes smoothly through the predominantly hardwood forest. You see small clearings and faint old roads. Then the trail enters the narrow valley of the Moose River's South Branch. After about two and a half hours of hiking, you reach the end of the truck trail in a large clearing. In dry weather you may wish to consider bicycling this far. It would offer a different dimension to the trip and relieve the tedium you may feel.

The trail, no longer maintained, crosses a stream on the east side of the clearing and passes through an area of spruce, balsam, and hemlock where many old logging roads converge. Insufficient marking makes it easy to lose your way among these faint old corridors. The trail turns right, heading back into open hardwoods, and as it begins to ascend, it turns left. If it is winter and you have skied in, you may want to change over to snowshoes here. The trail is obvious in some places, but blowdown and new growth have obscured it in others. For the rest of the way to the summit, you will follow a chaotic assortment of markers: red paint blazes, red tape, orange and silver reflective strips, and red DEC disks. After a gradual climb up a hill, a short descent takes you to two stream crossings and a beaver meadow, visible in the woods to the south. The trail now begins a steady, moderate climb in an easterly direction to the summit, where it levels off in mixed hardwoods and spruce.

After such a long journey, it is sad to behold the lonely tower, derelict and vandalized. Some of the steps are broken and it is unsafe to climb. This is unfortunate since the best views of the surrounding forest—in many cases, the only views—are from the tower. To the north, the ridges cradling the Fulton Chain Lakes trail off into the hills of the lower Moose River region. The Tug Hill Plateau with the Snow Ridge ski slopes near Turin is visible far to the northwest. The South Branch of the Moose River winds west past Remsen Falls, section 61, and to the southwest you can see an extension of Woodhull Lake. To the east, the rolling terrain surrounding the Moose River Plains leads your eye to the distant ranges of the West Canada Lakes Wilderness Area, a view encompassing some of the wildest lands in the state. Without the tower, views will be severely limited to a few rock outcrops. Red flagging to the north of the tower leads east to the Adirondack League Club boundary.

Remsen Falls

There is one positive note to observe on this long journey: this is the scene of one of the greatest triumphs of New York State conservationists, and one of the most significant Adirondack conservation battles of the past century.

From the northeast side of the clearing at the end of the truck trail, the old end of the railroad, you can, by careful searching and by staying on the west side of Raven Run, find the remains of the old access road that runs north 0.2 miles to the South Branch of the Moose. The South Branch at this point is a delightful, winding river where deer and beaver can frequently be seen. This scene that is so pleasant and tranquil was the proposed site of the Panther Dam. If it had been completed, the dam would have stretched north and south for 1800 feet across the river, rising to a maximum height of 175 feet. The impoundment would have flooded everything in the valley of the South Branch, upstream of this point and below an elevation of 1718 feet, a total of over 5000 acres, of which 900 were in the Forest Preserve.

The dam had been proposed at the urging of hydroelectric companies. The year 1919 saw the formation of the Black River Regulating District, which drew up plans to regulate fifty to sixty percent of the flow of the Black River and its tributaries through four huge dams. Under its direction, a dam was built at Stillwater on the Beaver. The proposed Higley Dam, further upstream on the Moose, was ultimately rejected; but in 1945 plans for the Panther site were being pushed by the Regulating District. By then it was obvious that regulating the Black was subservient to the desires for power. Many organizations, led by the Adirondack Mountain Club, fought the proposal, which was finally terminated in 1953. The state's voters rejected constitutional amendments to the Forest Preserve Law that would have permitted flooding of those lands. However, the fourth dam proposed, one at Hawkinsville on the Black River near Booneville, is still being considered. The battle to preserve New York's free-flowing, wild streams goes on.

61 Remsen Falls

Trail, hiking, camping, picnicking, cross-country skiing, fishing, swimming
3.4 miles, 1¼ hour, relatively level

You can make the trip to Remsen Falls in such short time because the route is mostly along the McKeever Truck Trail. Walk to the four-way intersection, 2.8 miles from the trailhead, where a blue-marked trail on the north descends for 0.5 mile to a clearing at a bend on the South Branch of the Moose River. If you look upriver, you can see Woodhull Mountain with its fire tower in the distance. In front of you, the river swings to the right and tumbles through a short, rocky course known as Remsen Falls. Below the falls, Nicks Creek joins the Moose from the northeast and the river turns sharply west. On the far bank above the confluence is the Remsen Falls lean-to, section 69. Fishermen's paths lead down past some campsites to various spots along the bank.

Toward the end of the 1700s, John Brown, a Connecticut businessman and Revolutionary War activist, came into possession of 210,000 acres of land in the upper Moose River-Fulton Chain region. Though it was a poor investment made in ignorance by his son-in-law, Brown was determined to exploit its possibilities. His surveyors constructed a road twenty-five miles long from Remsen to a point near where the Old Forge High School now stands. This was the first road to enter the wilderness from the southwest and it forded the South Branch in this area, hence the connection with the name of the falls. The road has disappeared now and we may only guess at the exact route it took. Fording the river today is difficult because of its width and the deep pools.

From the Moose River to Nicks Lake

THROUGH THIS AREA ran the final miles of one of the first roads to penetrate the Adirondack wilderness. After Connecticut businessman and Revolutionary War activist John Brown came into possession of 210,000 acres of remote, undeveloped acres to the north, his surveyors constructed an access road in from the southwest to a point along the Middle Branch of the Moose River between the Fulton Chain of Lakes and the confluence of the North Branch. Known as the Remsen Road because of its origin, it passed west of Woodhull Lake, crossed the Moose River's South Branch at Remsen Falls, and followed along Nicks Creek to Nicks Lake. It then passed over the intervening ridge, arriving at the "Brown's Tract" near the present site of the Old Forge School. The twenty-five-mile road, constructed in 1799 and 1800, was a tremendous accomplishment in these wild lands.

Decades passed and development of the Brown's Tract progressed painfully slowly, due to tragic personal setbacks and the stubborn north-woods climate. Other roads eventually entered the area from the west and northeast. For all these reasons, the Remsen Road fell into disuse. Slowly the woods claimed most of the route above North Lake Road, while pioneering efforts near Remsen rerouted some of the road and obscured the rest. Today, you can only imagine where this historic route went; time and many generations of lumbering have left little, if any, trace of its course.

There is, however, one place where you can travel through the quiet woods on, or at least near, the original route. The trail from Nicks Lake to Remsen Falls, section 69, follows Nicks Creek. As you hike along it, imagine the hearty settlers who passed north through this area to an uncertain future on the Brown's Tract. Interestingly, Alfred L. Donaldson in his *History of the Adirondacks,* quotes a document on the Brown's Tract by Charles E. Snyder, which states that this section of the Remsen Road followed "the old Indian Trail."

If indeed the Indians did have a trail here that predated the road, one individual who would surely have known was Nicholas Stoner. A native of Fulton County, "Nick" Stoner became one of the Adirondacks' most colorful personalities. An expert marksman, veteran of the American Revolution and the war of 1812, legendary Indian fighter, and tavern celebrity, he was also a dedicated husband, three times over. As a superior hunter and trapper, the vast wilderness to the north beckoned him and he ranged countless miles through the forest harvesting its bounty of furs, fish, and game. On one of his backwoods rambles he discovered a heretofore unknown lake. Like his contemporary, Jock Wright, who found "his" lake at modern Honnedaga, Nick boasted of his lake's beauty and bountiful game, but kept its location secret. Eventually, other woodsmen found it and Nick's Lake became public knowledge. Nick fared a bit better than Jock though, because today his name survives, having lost only the apostrophe. Section 65 details its features.

The Moose River roughly defines the northwestern edge of this region and it served as a major transportation route, both for lumber going out and vacationers and "sports" coming in. In 1889, a rickety little wooden railroad dubbed the "Peg Leg" carried an equally shaky little train seven miles from Moose River Settlement, four miles downstream from McKeever, to a point on the river named Minnehaha, near the present Singing Waters Campground. A log-and-board dam across the river here made it possible for steamboats to navigate upstream almost to Thendara. A lock and dam allowed the boats to continue up to a landing near the present location of the NY 28 bridge. This transportation system carried passengers for four years, then was discontinued. The upper dam is still in place, and you may either canoe or walk to it as described in sections 64 and 66.

Paralleling the river are the abandoned tracks of the Adirondack Railroad, discussed in earlier chapters. You will cross it to get to destinations described in sections 62 and 63. Old logging roads can be found running throughout the area and the trails you will walk have generally been routed along them.

62 Nelson Falls

Old road, paths, picnicking, swimming, fishing
0.5 mile, 10 minutes

The Moose River passes through a turbulent series of rapids and rocky steps at a bend 2.7 miles north of its confluence with the South Branch. Although it is not a falls in the true sense of the word, Nelson Falls commands the respect of whitewater enthusiasts who run this section and many chose to portage around it. During the dry summer months, however, it is an attractive spot with rocky slabs that invite picnicking and pools that beckon bathers and anglers. Giant cedars shelter the banks near the falls.

Nelson Falls

An old road turns right off NY 28, 2.8 miles north of the bridge at McKeever. It leads in 100 yards to a large parking area, then steadily descends past a gate. A second old road branches right at 0.1 mile and leads south to some camps. You should continue on the main route as it curves left and crosses the tracks of the Adirondack Railroad at 0.3 mile. Turn left and walk north along the tracks for a minute or two, then descend to the east to the river where you can follow fishermen's paths upstream to the falls. Not far above the falls, the railroad crosses the river on a bridge; and that is the way to go for access to paths and spots on the opposite bank. Part of the snowmobile trail system from Nicks Lake, section 67, runs along that bank and a short bushwhack south of the falls will intercept it.

63 Nelson Lake via the Moose River

Canoeing, fishing, swimming, picnicking, campsites

Below Nelson Falls, the Moose River changes its tempo and flows calmly for about three-quarters of a mile. Nelson Lake lies a half mile to the east and its wide outlet converges with the river here. By carrying a canoe down the old road used for the approach to Nelson Falls, you can easily launch into this waterway and enjoy a three-hour trip or a three-day outing.

Follow the old road east from the parking area, section 62, crossing the railroad tracks at 0.3 mile. A path on the opposite side leads down and to the right and brings you out at a side channel of the river. You can launch here, but there is a beaver dam where it reenters the river. To avoid it, you will have to carry a little further down the bank to a second launching point, where there may be some overturned rowboats.

A lazy current carries you along this section, and there are signs of beaver and muskrat. Herd paths approach the water's edge and a variety of tracks can be discovered. Ducks and great blue herons frequently rise up from along the grassy banks, and belted kingfishers and cedar waxwings swoop through the air overhead.

One half mile downstream, the river bends right and after another one-fifth of a mile, it drops to a series of rapids that continue all the way to the confluence with the South Branch. Turn left at the bend and you will be pointed into the Nelson Lake outlet. As you paddle into this quarter-mile-long channel, you may notice blue trail markers off in the woods to the right. These mark a trail that is part of a long loop system running through the center of this northernmost section of the Black River Wild Forest Area, sections 65 and 68 through 70.

Nelson Lake

You paddle to the right of a marshy backwater area, then the channel narrows and, in midsummer, is filled with pickerel-weed. You can easily negotiate around the few rocks and logs at the outlet, which soon opens up into the lake itself. Your eye is drawn up the length of the lake to the northeast where the wooded dome of Little Roundtop rises in the distance. Red-tailed hawks patrol the skies above and you may see a playful otter bobbing in the water near a swampy bay to the right. The southeastern shore becomes rugged and large rocks extend out into the water. The northwest shore is brushy in places and blue flag irises are found there in early summer. A few stands of conifers lie in the lower, wet areas, but the forest cover is dominated by mature hardwoods and several campsites can be found beneath them along the lake's perimeter.

A choice spot for swimming, picnicking, and relaxing in the sun exists at the lake's northern end, to the right of a swampy section. A sandy beach and a large slab of rock entice you to stop for a while and enjoy the peace and beauty of your surroundings. There is a campsite just back in the woods and an easy bushwhack north along herd paths can take you to the trail system, sections 67 and 68.

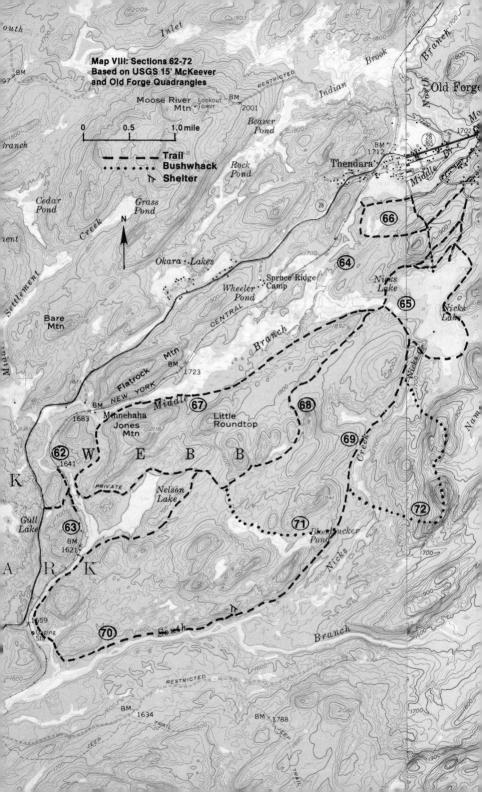

Map VIII: Sections 62-72
Based on USGS 15' McKeever
and Old Forge Quadrangles

0   0.5   1.0 mile

- – – Trail
· · · · Bushwhack
⌂ Shelter

64 Canoeing the Moose River

You will seldom find a canoe trip so close to a developed area that offers such a wilderness-quality experience as the Moose River does south of NY 28. From the hamlets of Thendara and Old Forge, the river follows a sinuous course southwest and you will find at least 6 river miles of flatwater paddling. Extensive, grassy wetlands border much of the way and most creatures indigenous to the Adirondack forest can be seen here. The rewards are great if you paddle slowly and silently, starting, perhaps, at dawn when animal activity is high and continuing through the day.

The best access point is found by turning onto Fourth Street in Thendara. It is the first street branching south from NY 28 on the north side of the railroad overpass. Follow it for 0.5 mile and cross a bridge over the river. Turn sharp right and park at the trailhead for the snowmobile trails described in section 66. There is room for several cars here and you may put your canoe in from the banks near the bridge.

Heading down river, you immediately enter a widened section with a beaver lodge. Great blue heron frequently feed here among the patches of pickerel-weed and marsh grass. Some homes stand along the north shore and old large buildings tell of a more prosperous past. The river narrows and closely parallels the railroad tracks to the right. Twenty minutes into your trip, you reach the wooden dam and spillway that once made steamer traffic between McKeever and Thendara possible. The lock, however, is no longer there. It is easy to carry around the dam, but you must do so on the left bank since the land on the right bank is private. There is a clearing with campsites on the left side and a snowmobile trail leads from here to the trail network near Nicks Lake, section 66.

Below the dam, the river wanders for about 4 miles, interrupted only by two or three shallow riffles. Let the current guide you and paddle only to steer or avoid obstacles. As you round each bend, have your binoculars and camera ready. Finally, near the base of Flatrock Mountain, shallow rapids form and it is time to turn back.

Above the Fourth Street Bridge, you can continue to paddle along the marshy channel, coming to NY 28 in a mile. Flatwater continues upstream from the highway and can be followed up the North and Middle Branches of the Moose to adventures described in *Discover the West Central Adirondacks*.

Moose River looking toward Nelson Lake

65 Nicks Lake

Trail, hiking, cross-country skiing, camping, swimming, fishing, picnicking, canoeing
4.5 miles, 1¾ hours, relatively level

Nicks Lake lies south of Thendara. Its state-owned shoreline includes a DEC campground on the east. To reach it, turn from NY 28 on the west side of the high school in Old Forge and follow the DEC signs out of the village to the Bisby Road, and then turn right at the campground entrance. A shorter approach is to take Fourth Street in Thendara, section 64, across the Moose River, then turn sharp left and continue 0.4 mile, taking your first right. This is Joy Tract Road and it leads steeply up to Bisby Road in 0.25 mile. The road beyond leads to the private holdings of the Adirondack League Club.

Nicks Lake Campground has excellent camping, swimming, and picnicking facilities, and since no motorized watercraft are permitted, it is relatively quiet. A trail encircles the lake and gives access to the features described in the rest of this chapter. A fee is charged for use of the facilities, but for those who are hiking beyond the campground, free parking is available at two locations. The first is just beyond the entrance booth, after you turn right, onto Loop A Road. A parking area is on the right and a register is just down the road where a short blue-marked trail leads to the trail around the lake. You may also turn left beyond the booth and drive all the way in to the large parking lot near the beach and picnic area. The description of the lake trail will begin here.

From the parking area, head south to a register and signboard in the trees at the far end of the beach. Following yellow markers through a tall woods, you quickly cross a major inlet on an elaborate, floating bridge. Canoes may pass under this bridge and enter the small wetland to the left where there is a traditional loon nesting area. No nesting took place in 1986, perhaps because well-meaning, but curious individuals disturbed them during the critical nesting season.

The trail reenters the woods and passes through a hemlock stand with painted trillium and pink lady's slippers underfoot here in spring. At 0.7 mile there is a sturdy new bridge over Nicks Creek. Beyond the trail climbs steeply along an old road for 0.1 mile to a junction with another road that is part of the long blue-marked loop trail. A left turn here will take you to Remsen Falls, section 69, then on along the South Branch of the Moose River, section 70. The trail then passes Nelson Lake and rejoins the Nicks Lake Trail, section 68.

Turning right, you head north-northwest, following both yellow and blue trail markers, as well as snowmobile trail markers, through mature hardwoods with a few wet sections. You see the lake occasionally through the trees and in less than ten minutes, a faint path leads right past a campsite to the lake's shore. The trail swings away from the lake and after another ten minutes, you reach a junction with yet another old road, 1.8 miles from the trailhead. The blue-marked loop trail and a snowmobile trail come in from Nelson Lake and the Moose River on the left, and you should turn right to continue around the lake. A clearing is seen to the left and the trail is now wide and grassy.

Just over fifteen minutes later, at the 2.5-mile point, the yellow-marked lake trail forks right. The old road, with its blue and snowmobile markers, continues on for another mile to a trailhead register and signboard on the

Bisby Road, 300 yards from the intersection with Joy Tract Road. Following the right fork, you descend slightly for 0.2 mile and come to a junction with an old road. A right turn will take you 100 yards to a campsite at the lake. The way left is full of blowdown, but it leads 300 yards north to the blue-marked snowmobile trail. Continuing straight ahead, the yellow-marked trail narrows and, after 0.3 mile, comes to another junction with an old road. This one marks the boundary of the campgrounds and to the right, it leads 0.2 mile to the lake; to the left, it goes 0.3 mile to the blue-marked snowmobile trail.

You now enter a most attractive area, where the trail crosses a stream then pitches up through tall white pines. The lake is again visible to the right and the blue-marked side trail from Loop A Road comes in on the left. A pump house on the lake's edge is seen and the trail continues along its scenic course through tall trees dominated by hemlocks. The various loops of campsites now approach on the left and you soon cross a gravel road leading to another pump house. You eventually come out on Loop E Road, and trail signs direct you along it back to the parking lot.

66 Snowmobile Trails North of Nicks Lake
Hiking, cross-country skiing, picnicking, camping

These trails are, in themselves, not very interesting, but they are short and may be used as alternate routes of access to areas already described. They converge high on a hilltop and so provide skiers with a few downhill runs. All follow old roads and are currently well marked and maintained.

Just after crossing the Fourth Street Bridge, section 64, you will notice a parking area and a trailhead on the right. A wide trail heads west, paralleling (but out of sight of) the Moose River. You pass an old clearing and at 0.5 mile a side trail that leads right 0.1 mile to a clearing on the river bank near the old lock and dam. There is room to picnic and camp here and the area is heavily used. The main trail swings away from the river and slowly ascends as it curves to the east. It ends at a junction with the other trails near the top of the hill, 1.6 miles from its start.

Another trail, 0.9 mile in length, also leaves this trailhead and follows an old road from Thendara to the north shore of Nicks Lake. Heading due south, it ascends moderately to a junction near some large pines at 0.4 mile. The trail left slowly descends 0.6 mile to a gate at Bisby Road, 0.1 mile from the intersection with Joy Tract Road. Continuing straight ahead, you pass some clearings on the left after 200 feet and the trail from the lock and dam enters on the right. A brief level stretch follows, then a 0.2-mile drop to the trail coming in from Bisby Road Trailhead, 300 yards from the Joy Tract Road intersection. The trail officially ends here, but straight ahead you can see the path of the old road, filled with blowdown. You can follow it 300 yards to where it crosses the Nicks Lake Trail, section 65, then continue another 100 yards to the lake.

67 Moose River Snowmobile Trail
Hiking, cross-country skiing
4.6 miles, 2 hours, relatively level

This trail leaves the Nicks Lake Trail, section 65, at a point 1.8 miles from the trailhead near the beach. It is a continuation of the blue-marked hiking and snowmobile trail originating at the Bisby Road Trailhead, section 66. The latter approach is more desirable because it is 1.7 miles long and relatively level. Many varieties of ferns fill the trail and the mature hardwood forest is attractive, but the way is uneventful and even boring for hiking. Skiers may even find the route tedious because there is little variation in terrain. Nevertheless, it does provide a link to the Moose River near Nelson Falls and it can be used as part of several loop options.

Leaving the Nicks Lake Trail, you head southwest for 0.2 mile to a junction where the snowmobile trail splits. Turn right and follow occasional markers as the trail slowly descends west-southwest, gradually approaching the Moose River. Within 1 mile, at a point the trail bends sharply right, you will see a beaver-flooded area through the trees to the left, a handsome enough spot for a detour. The trail crosses a few wet areas beyond the bend, and after 2.5 miles the cover becomes predominantly evergreens as you enter the lowlands along the river. Through the trees to the right you can see Flatrock Mountain behind open wetlands.

For 1 mile, you walk quite close to the river. Then, turning south, you begin to ascend through a draw between Jones Mountain on the east and an unnamed hill to the west. The trail becomes excessively wet and is very difficult to walk. Finally, a gradual descent leads to a clearing on the Moose River, just below Nelson Falls. A short mile bushwhack upstream takes you to paths along the river that lead past the falls, and 0.5 mile from the clearing you reach the railroad bridge where you can cross the river and head out to NY 28, 0.7 mile away, section 62.

The snowmobile trail continues east past the clearing, 1.6 miles to a junction with the blue-marked loop trail, section 68, which it then follows northeast to Nicks Lake. After passing through a draw, it curves around the northern edge of Nelson Lake, which is occasionally visible through the trees. The trail crosses two major streams in this stretch, and just past the second one, a hunter's path heads south to the nice campsite near the water described in section 63. The trail then steadily ascends for 0.4 mile to the junction.

68 Nelson Lake

Snowmobile trail, hiking, cross-country skiing, campsites, swimming
3.8 miles, 2 hours, relatively level

This trail is similar in character to the Moose River snowmobile trail, section 67. It is maintained also as a hiking trail and is part of a long loop that returns to Nicks Lake via the South Branch of the Moose River and the trail to Remsen Falls. Many old logging roads intersect the trail and an occasional non-native Scotch pine indicates the timbering disturbances this region felt. A few wet beaver-flooded sections may impede your progress.

Leaving the Nicks Lake Trail, section 65, you head southwest, following blue hiking and orange snowmobile markers to a junction at 0.2 mile where the Moose River snowmobile trail forks right. Continue straight ahead through the mature hardwoods, passing in half an hour a flooded area with dead standing timber on the left. After a slight ascent, the trail reaches a height-of-land and you begin a long, gradual descent, passing a large vly on the right at 2.1 miles.

At the 2.8-mile point, about one hour and twenty minutes after you leave the Nicks Lake Trail, you may notice a faded wooden trail sign high up on a tree on the right side of the trail. This indicates the former junction of the abandoned snowmobile trail from Bloodsucker Pond, section 71, and careful searching in the woods opposite the sign will reveal the old road that it followed.

The Nelson Lake Trail now swings northwest and continues to descend over a rerouted section. The old trail runs off to the left. You cross a stream in the clearing of an old, dried-up beaver pond, beyond which the old trail comes in from the left, joining the newer route. At 3.4 miles, you reach a junction where the Moose River snowmobile trail comes in from the right. It is 0.4 mile down this trail to the upper end of Nelson Lake, section 63. The blue-marked hiking trail forks left and leads past the Nelson Lake outlet and Moose River in 1.5 miles, then continues on to the South Branch, section 70.

69 Remsen Falls
Trail, hiking, lean-to, cross-country skiing, swimming
3.8 miles, 1½ hours from Nicks Lake Trail junction, relatively level

From its junction with the Nicks Lake Trail, section 65, this wide, grassy trail gradually descends south-southwest, following blue hiking and orange snowmobile trail markers. It is a popular route and well defined as it passes through the mature hardwood forest. After ten minutes, it begins to narrow and passes a spring with a pipe and a wooden trough on the right. The well-posted Adirondack League Club boundary approaches on the left, then turns away after a few yards. Nicks Creek is occasionally visible through the trees to the left. You cross another stream after twenty-five minutes and soon loose sight of the creek as the trail winds through the woods, where you cross a few intermittent streams.

One hour and 2.3 miles from the Nicks Lake Trail, an old junction is reached. You may see faded fragments of old wooden signs on the ground, and the keen-eyed hiker might see where an old snowmobile trail, section 71, turned right away from the hiking trail. It led to Bloodsucker Pond and beyond to the trail near Nelson Lake. Five minutes past this junction, you cross the tumbling outlet of Bloodsucker Pond. As you contour along the side of a ridge, this attractive section of trail passes through fern-covered areas with many boulders. The trail becomes relatively level and the mixed woods takes on an even, orderly appearance. Soon you come to the alder-choked end of Nicks Creek where it empties into the South Branch of the Moose River, and in a small clearing above this confluence, sits the lean-to. It faces upstream toward the boulder-filled drop in the river known as Remsen Falls.

70 Remsen Falls-Nelson Lake Link Trail
Hiking
3.9 miles, 2 hours to Nelson Lake Outlet

The blue-marked trail continues past the Remsen Falls lean-to, swinging west and paralleling the South Branch of the Moose River. It is fairly well defined, but not used as much as other trails and therefore takes on a more primitive character.

Beyond the lean-to, you come close to the river where you cross a stream. The trail then rises high above the water, and you walk with through-the-trees glimpses of the scenic rock-filled river below. Soon the forest thickens and you lose sight of the river. After crossing an exposed section of bed-rock, the trail gradually begins to lose elevation. At 2.0 miles, a wide swing north-northwest takes you to the edge of the Moose River, 0.2 mile above its confluence with the South Branch.

The trail follows close to the river, which is a continuous stretch of rocky rapids. On the opposite bank, you will see the railroad tracks running parallel to, and high above, the water. After crossing a stream, the trail slowly turns northeast and proceeds along an old logging road that is quite grown in and wet in places. Conditions eventually improve and you come to what appears to be the remains of an old rock dam. Behind it, the river widens into the slack water into which the outlet of Nelson Lake flows, section 63.

The trail continues on another 1.5 miles to a junction with the Moose River snowmobile trail, section 67. Following an old logging road through this section, it swings away from Nelson Lake, then gradually ascends north-east through an area where many faint old roads can be seen. Past the junction, the combined trails head northeast to the Nicks Lake Trail, section 68.

71 Bloodsucker Pond
Bushwhack, abandoned snowmobile trail

One hour along the Remsen Falls Trail, section 69, at a point 2.3 miles from the Nicks Lake Trail, there is a faint junction. A snowmobile trail used to head west 0.3 mile to Bloodsucker Pond, then turned northwest paralleling a major inlet. It then swung north and connected with the trail to Nelson Lake, section 68. It followed an old road for much, if not all, of its 1.6 miles and although it has been abandoned for ten years, enough remains for the bushwhacker to follow. Bloodsucker Pond is a worthy destination in itself.

The junction is fading fast, but you may be able to locate it by sighting remains of the wooden signs that were once posted here. The trail itself is choked with beech saplings and viburnums and it is hard to follow. If you cannot find the junction, just continue down the trail a few minutes until you come to the outlet. The pond sits 100 feet higher than the trail and its outlet tumbles over several small cascades. A natural rock dam holds back its waters, and current beaver activity may raise it further. The major inlet approaches from the northwest, then bends sharply northeast below

another rock dam. Brushy wetlands line the inlet for most of its length, and a beaver dam crosses it just above the main body of the pond. Aside from the beavers, many other animals and birds live here, and it is a peaceful place to spend some time observing nature.

72 Cliffs Southeast of Nicks Lake
Bushwhack, limited views

The view from these cliffs is less than spectacular and the bushwhack is not easy, but it is about the only view in this area. For those who enjoy traveling far from the beaten path, as Nick Stoner must have, this trip will be more than satisfying. With the 5.4-mile distance and the 500-foot vertical rise, this becomes a strenuous trip that requires the stamina of the old-time trappers. If you want to take time to enjoy the views on the way, allow nearly six hours for the trip.

Begin by hiking down the Remsen Falls Trail, section 69, to the well-blazed and well-posted boundary line of the Adirondack League Club, which comes in from the east. The trail follows this boundary for a short ways to a corner where the line turns southeast. Leave the trail at this corner and descend along the line, staying to the right of it on state land. In five minutes, you will be at the edge of a brushy wetland along Nicks Creek. Except in winter, this spot is difficult to cross, so you will have to bushwhack downstream a quarter mile to cross on an old beaver dam.

Once across the creek, the boundary ascends steeply. There are fewer signs, but blazes are usually visible and they will take you through the hardwood forest to the top of a ridge. Leaving the boundary line, bushwhack south-southwest along the ridge to the highest point where a large boulder gives you your first view east-northeast toward Little Moose Mountain. Continue south-southwest, dropping to a draw where you should turn toward magnetic south to a second high point. Staying just east of the ridge line, follow it as it curves southwest and several outcrops will present themselves. The views are east-southeast, looking up the valley of the Moose River's South Branch, and they extend to the south-southeast toward Woodhull Mountain.

When the ridge no longer has views and you are just above the canopy of the hardwood forest, set your return route toward magnetic northwest. Your descent will not be difficult and you will intercept Nicks Creek where it is narrow and easily crossed. Continue northwest to the Remsen Falls Trail, turn right, and Nicks Lake is forty-five minutes away.

Otter Lake-White Lake Trails

EXCEPT FOR A few small parcels spilling over the Herkimer County line between Otter Lake and Hinckley Reservoir, a small tract of land west of NY 28 constitutes Oneida County's portion of the Adirondack Forest Preserve. Three small lakes lined with many camps are found here. The southernmost is White Lake, whose entire shoreline is privately owned. To the northwest lies Long Lake, similar in shape and geologic origin to the much larger and well-known lake of the same name in the center of the Park. Public access for canoeing and fishing can be found by turning off NY 28 at the sharp bend south of White Lake onto Round Lake Road. Travel 0.6 mile to Long Lake Road and follow it north 1.1 miles to a junction where Capron Road comes in from the right. You are now on state land; there is room for four or five cars to park on the right. A short path on the left leads 25 feet to shore.

Farther north on NY 28 is the settlement of Otter Lake on the eastern edge of its watery namesake. A levee on the lake's outlet provides the best location for public access. Turn left off NY 28, 0.35 mile north of the flashing lights in the village onto Lakeview Road. Follow it 1.4 miles to the end of pavement and the beginning of state land. There is room to park here and the outlet is 0.1 mile down the dirt extension of the road.

The Adirondack Division of the New York Central Railroad served this area near the turn of the century. One spur led to the shore of White Lake, where ice was harvested and sent to Utica. Generations of logging left their mark on the adjacent woods. Today, many old tote roads can be found coursing through the hardwood-covered hills. The DEC has laid out a system of snowmobile trails along some of these old roads. They provide peaceful hiking routes in summer, and, unless there is heavy snowmobile traffic, they make excellent cross-country ski routes. Despite an occasional mudhole, the trails are as a rule, well maintained. They are also well marked, albeit with a potpourri of yellow, orange, and red snowmobile trail markers, some of which are quite faded and brittle. Pay close attention to them since many old tote roads intersect the trails.

73 Brandy Lake from Round Lake Road
Snowmobile trail
2.6 miles, 1½ hours, 100-foot vertical rise

This southernmost of the region's trails is the least attractive because of its muddy spots. Vehicular intrusions have hastened this deterioration and vehicular use of intervening tote roads causes temporary confusion at some junctions. Access is from Round Lake Road, 1.1 miles from its intersection with NY 28.

The first 0.6 mile of trail lies on private property owned by the Masonic Home of Utica. The trail passes through small open areas and soon joins a dirt road coming in from the left. Markers are scarce, but you should spot one on the left side. An old trail branches off to the left through a lumber clearing and reenters the woods again. It is no longer maintained. Stay on the dirt road which is the newer trail. You enter state land, then descend to the point where the old trail comes in from the left. A wetland is visible to the northwest.

Beaver-flooded Trail to Brandy Lake

After hiking an easy mile, you turn sharply left. The trail descends to cross the outlet of a murky pond. The dam of a long-gone beaver colony still remains, butted up against the right side of the bridge and rising three feet above it. Overflow has eroded the area and the going is wet and awkward.

Beyond the bridge you ascend to a small clearing with a fire ring. Straight ahead is a well-used tote road. The trail makes an abrupt left turn and you begin to head west. Passing a small wetland on the left, you gradually swing to the northeast and begin to climb on a muddy, eroded section, gaining eighty feet in the next 0.2 mile.

The trail levels off, a few large mudholes are passed and around the 2-mile point, a tote road goes straight ahead while the trail turns sharply to the right. Within 0.5 mile of Brandy Lake, blowdown has put an end to motorized passage, but the mudholes persist. Near the lake, the trail improves and becomes the easy route to Otter Lake you can enjoy in section 74.

74 Otter Lake Outlet Trail

Snowmobile trail, cross-country skiing
1.6 miles, 1 hour, relatively level

On the west side of NY 28, 1.7 miles south of the flashing lights in Otter Lake village, there is a parking turnoff for access to snowmobile trails in the area. A single broad trail heads northwest from the turnout and descends to a bridge across the brushy outlet of Otter Lake at 0.4 mile. Just beyond, the trail ascends a steep pitch and at 0.5 mile comes to a junction.

The trail left continues on another 1.7 miles to Brandy Lake, section 75. If you turn right, you head northeast through a level, rocky section with rock outcrops on the left. A gradual descent takes you to the edge of the outlet. This is a most attractive stretch; the waters flow over a rocky course through a peaceful, mixed woods. The trail passes a few wet spots, then swings away from the outlet, shortly reaching another junction where a spur trail leads right for 0.3 mile to Woods Road and NY 28. Continue ahead for 0.1 mile and you reach the levee and the spillway at Otter Lake's outlet.

Map IX: Sections 53-55, 73-77
Based on USGS 15' McKeever Quadrangle

Path
Trail
Jeep Road

75 Brandy Lake from NY 28

Snowmobile trail, camping, hunting, cross-country skiing
2.2 miles, 1¼ hour, 100-foot vertical rise

The best part of a trip to Brandy Lake is just that, the hike itself. The trail is broad and smooth with a few modest grades and only subtle changes in the scenery. The lake has a brushy shoreline and it is difficult to find a good lookout over the lake near the trail. This is a popular destination with hunters. The number of clearings in the corridors of old tote roads lend themselves to fine campsites. Skiers will find the brushy shores no impediment to enjoying the frozen surfaces of the lake.

From the junction with the Otter Lake Outlet Trail, section 74, 0.5 miles from NY 28, head southwest along the grassy woods road. Wetlands along the outlet appear through the trees to the left. The road gradually swings 180° to the right allowing you to see Long Lake to the southwest. Another 180° swing, this one to the left, begins with a pitch down to the bridge crossing the outlet of Lost Pond. You begin a gradual ascent and quickly come to the junction with the trail to Round Pond at 1.1 miles, section 77. Continuing southwest, you pass rock formations on the right. As you make the gradual climb, there is another brief view of Long Lake off to the left.

The trail now levels off and narrows slightly before sloping down to cross the outlet of Brandy Lake. A large sprocket lies rusting on the left side of the trail, a reminder of the time when the woods yielded to mechanization. A small vly is seen upstream and you begin a slight ascent, crossing another stream in just a few minutes. Cresting a knoll, you dip down to a wet area and recross the outlet. The lake soon appears through the trees to the left.

76 Lost Pond

Path, camping, hunting

The route described here actually takes you to two ponds which, at first glance, are not very attractive. But together with their outlet's wetland, they provide the ideal habitat for common Adirondack wildlife. Hunters know this well since they have made several informal campsites and marked the path between the ponds that you will follow.

Lakeview Road circles the north and west sides of Otter Lake. From the parking area at the end of Lakeview Road, walk back up the pavement 200 yards and find an old road entering on the north side. Follow this road west-southwest and in fifteen minutes you will be in the vicinity of the first pond. Ahead, the road fades and there are a few campsites with connecting footpaths. Bearing right, toward the wetland, you will find a path marked with red paint and can covers. This will take you to the edge of the first pond, a murky, brushy body of water with many pond lilies.

The path crosses the outlet, which is incorrectly shown on the topo map as coming from the south end of the pond. The north end has dead, standing timber, and an old beaver lodge. The western shore is steep with a few rocks along the edge.

77 Round Pond

Snowmobile trail, camping, cross-country skiing
2.5 miles, 1¼ hours, 160-foot descent

To reach the trailhead to Round Pond, drive north on NY 28 from Otter Lake to McKeever to the bridge over the Moose River. Just south of the bridge, Moose River Road turns off to the west, left. Drive 2.2 miles down Moose River Road to a point where the snowmobile trail enters from the south. Since there is no turnout here, you will have to park on the narrow shoulder. From the road, it is a short ascent of 0.25 mile to an unmarked junction where a spur trail forks right. It leads in less than 0.1 mile to an informal campsight on the eastern edge of Round Pond. The shoreline is boggy and difficult to walk along. Across the pond from the campsite is a beaver lodge and signs of fresh beaver work.

The trail continues south beyond Round Pond, climbing to a height-of-land in the next 0.5 mile. After a level stretch, you notice through the trees that the land to the east seems to drop away. You now begin a moderate descent and cross two streams. The trail levels off and 2.5 miles from Moose River Road intersects the trail to Brandy Lake from NY 28, section 75. With a car at each end, this would make a short, enjoyable cross-country ski trip with a challenging downhill run in the middle. The route can also be combined with either the Brandy Lake or Otter Lake Outlet trails, sections 75 and 74.

Independence River Wild Forest

THE INDEPENDENCE RIVER Wild Forest holds down the westernmost flank of the Adirondack Park. If you are traveling from west to east, the Wild Forest is your gateway to the western Adirondacks, technically known as the Adirondack Hill Country.

The Wild Forest's western boundary places you astride a line separating civilization from wilderness. If you face westward, you look over an escarpment (elevation 1250 feet) into the Black River Valley (elevation 750 feet) where you find a continuous string of villages stretching from Boonville northward through Lowville to Carthage. If you look eastward, you face a dense forest that marks the beginning of the Adirondacks. The transition from one to the other is as striking as it is sudden.

The Independence River region inside the Forest Preserve has been classified Wild Forest because of its many roads and private inholdings. This classification means that roads, man-made structures, and motorized vehicles such as snowmobiles and all-terrain vehicles are allowed in parts of the state land.

Although it is part of the Adirondack Hill region, the land making up the Independence River Wild Forest is relatively level, while sloping gently upwards as you move from west to east. As a result, much of the Wild Forest's low spots and depressions are wet and boggy. Its creeks and streams flow westward, eventually draining into the Black River.

The two largest and best-known waterways are Otter Creek and the Independence River. Both are attractive streams displaying eye-catching falls throughout their entire length. The Independence, which is classified as a Scenic River, is the longer of the two, twenty-eight miles, and the more remote. Its headwaters are found just south of the hamlet of Big Moose.

Otter Creek, which traces its headwaters to Big Otter Lake, is only sixteen miles long. Because it is relatively easy to reach and well stocked with brown trout, Otter Creek attracts avid trout anglers to its banks, making it the area's most popular fishing stream.

The Independence loops north while the Otter swings south through the Wild Forest, approaching each other outside the Park's western boundary. They are but a mile apart when they enter the Black River. If you drive north from Greig for 1.3 miles on Pine Grove Road, you can sample them both in a short space. Other access points outside the Park are found on Erie Canal Road and Eatonville Road, where a spot south of the bridge over the Independence River offers a private picnic and camping area for which a fee is charged.

Trout, both browns and brookies, are found in virtually all of the area's streams as well as its many ponds. The names of the many streams range from the commonplace to the unusual. In the north you will find Lizard Spring Brook, Sunday Creek, Hitchcock Creek, Hay Creek, and Second, Third, Fourth, and Fifth creeks.

In the central sector, you encounter Beaver Meadow Creek and the Independence River, while in the south you can fish Tommy Roaring, Otter, Pine, Fish, and Drunkard creeks and Poison Brook.

While there are no mountains to climb in the Wild Forest, you do find rapidly changing land forms—from sand dunes in the west to small hills with bedrock outcrops and erratics (rounded boulders dropped off by the retreating glacier) in the east, and from small ponds in the western quarter to wetland and beaver impoundments in the central region.

The western part of the Wild Forest is surprisingly flat. It becomes more irregular to the east, rising to small hills in the far east. Stillwater Mountain (elevation 2264 feet) where you will find a fire tower, is located a short distance west of Stillwater Reservoir. Big Pico Mountain (elevation 1666 feet) and Little Pico Mountain (elevation 1640 feet) are found in the southeastern part of the Wild Forest. These are the local names for these two hills, so you will not find them on any official map.

GLACIERS SHAPED THE LAND

The entire region has been glaciated, leaving a mantle of relatively course till and outwash to form numerous ponds and low areas that have become today's swamps and bogs. The widespread sand deposits north of Brantingham Lake are glacial river deltas that flowed into the Glenville Stage and Port Leyden Stage of the glacial lake that occupied the Black River valley during the recession of the Wisconsin Advance in the late Pleistocene Epoch. In the western section around the Chase Lake area, you find a sand plain, brought here by streams—today's Independence River and Otter Creek—during the retreat of the last continental glacier, which had covered virtually all of the state. When the retreating glacier stalled around the Watertown area, it blocked the northerly flow of the Black River, producing a large impoundment with water rising over the escarpment and flooding the Chase Lake area.

When the sand-filled waters coming down from the central Adirondacks met the waters of the impoundment, they slowed and deposited their content. When the glacier continued its retreat, the waters of the impoundment lowered, leaving behind a sand plain running from Crystal Lake in the north to what is called the Sand Flats State Forest in the south.

Rivers flowing from the east have cut deeply through the sand plains, their valleys creating most of the region's major elevation changes. The deep valleys cut by the Independence and Otter approach 300 feet near the Park's western boundary. Because the glacial soil has relatively little ability to hold water, the rivers are raging torrents during snow-melt and heavy rains, but almost dry streams in midsummer.

The Wild Forest has a history of limited farming, heavy logging, and several devastating forest fires. The land still shows the effects of these man-made incursions, especially around the Chase Lake area, where you find vast acreages of open land. On some the topsoil was so severely eroded by man's activities that only mosses and lichens cover the soil. Vast fields of dense meadow-sweet, a bush in the spirea family, are occasionally being covered with aspen, black cherry, pin cherry, and shadbush. These areas of Colton Sands have been especially slow to regenerate.

There are over eighty individual ponds and lakes to enhance the area's varied landscape and aquatic environments. The largest body of water is Stillwater Reservoir, which is nine miles long, two miles wide, with seventy miles of shoreline. Because of the access it provides to the Wilderness areas to the north, the most eastern portion of the Wild Forest is included in *Discover the Northwestern Adirondacks*. Big and Little Otter and Francis lakes are all within the Forest Preserve. Private lakes in or near the Wild Forest include Crystal, Chase, and Brantingham.

The area was heavily lumbered well into the 1920s, and although the forest has reclaimed much of the land, the trees are young, second growth. Originally settlers of the 1820s moved into the Black River Valley and up the escarpment into today's Wild Forest to farm. However, they quickly saw that the sale of lumber was going to bring them more money than farming. Soon large log drives took place on all the major west-flowing streams. Seasonally, logs were floated down the Independence and Otter into the Black River and then northward to Carthage where the St. Regis

Paper Company was located. When the Black River Canal reached Lyons Falls in 1856, a new route to market was opened to the south via the Erie Canal. NY 12 north of Boonville follows the route of this marvelously narrow canal with its 109 locks. Roadside stops let you study the remains of a few of them.

Sawmills sprang up at every available waterfall on the Independence River and Otter Creek. Around those mills, small communities arose taking the names of the mill owners—Carterville, Partridgeville, Botchfordville, and Dolgeville. All have vanished, though the names are preserved in road names.

Richard Carter ran a sawmill on Otter Creek, cutting shingles, laths, and fence pickets. At its peak, the mill employed 75 people. The community of Carterville later became Eatonville. Charles Partridge employed twenty-five people in his mill which was also located on the Otter Creek. The last mill to be located on Otter Creek was built on the John Brown Tract by the Keltys of New York City. This mill sawed lumber for the manufacture of piano sounding boards. A tannery employing forty to fifty people also operated on Otter Creek.

THE REGION'S APPEAL

Geographically, the Wild Forest divides from north to south into three areas corresponding to the geological and ecological differences. As you discover the differences of each, you will note one common thread. The western portion of each is easily accessible by a network of interconnected dirt and sand roads which in wintertime become part of the region's 100-mile network of marked snowmobile trails. In summer some of these routes may be used legally by all-terrain vehicles. As you move further east, these trails become fewer and more foot trails appear. However, most of the foot travel is done on roads that allow you to reach all the major lakes and ponds and the banks of virtually every stream.

The roads exist primarily because they provide access to the region's private inholdings and they lead to different kinds of use from most of the rest of the Adirondacks. Two kinds of outdoor people will enjoy these western roads. Those who need vehicular access will find that the roads lead to several lovely destinations. This guide details carefully which roads are open and which are closed. Hunters and fishermen, who are currently the principal users of the area, will continue to find access through this road network.

These roads have another benefit—those who need a firm, flat trail for walking will find such trails here as nowhere else in the Adirondacks. The guide describes which roads make good hiking, which are covered with

Lake Francis

a closed-tree canopy to provide summer shade, and where open areas occur for birding. Birding is especially good in this region, and no one spot seems to be better than others. The openness of the road system makes birds easy to spot and the bogs and wetlands are especially productive. The New York State Breeding Bird Atlas lists 120 probable or confirmed breeding species. On trips into the area, both barred and great-horned owls were sighted, as well as loons, ravens, and herons. Thrushes, vireos, and warblers abound in late spring.

Note that most of the network of dirt roads is not plowed in winter and is used as part of the snowmobile trail network. In some areas, snowmobile use has declined sufficiently that the DEC will no longer maintain some trails. Much of the time, you can ski on the snowmobile trails, though you must use caution and give way to the machines. There are only short sections listed exclusively for skiers. Most of the distant foot trails could be skied, but they are so remote that they would only be accessible on winter camping expeditions.

The roads will do one more thing: their names will amuse and intrigue you. Nowhere else in the Adirondacks does there seem to be such a wealth of unusual names. Who could resist exploring a Confusion Flats Road, or an Extra Road, or a Useless Road?

Independence River

Brantingham Lake Area

THE SOUTHERN APPROACH to the Independence River Wild Forest along Brantingham Road takes you into a thick woods that continues east, almost unbroken to the Ha-de-ron-dah Wilderness. The road leads first to Brantingham Lake, a community of summer homes just outside the Wild Forest but within the "blue line" that marks the boundary of the Park.

You reach the Brantingham Lake area from NY 12, which runs north-south between Utica and Watertown. Turn right, east, from NY 12, at Burdick Crossing Road, 5 miles north of Lyons Falls. Drive east, across the Black River to the intersection with Lyons Falls Road. Turn left and drive 0.5 mile north through the hamlet of Greig to the intersection with Brantingham Road. Turn right on it for 5 miles past the Brantingham Inn Motel (on the left) to an intersection, which is just short of Brantingham Lake itself.

At the intersection, blacktop Brantingham Road forks into two dirt roads. The northern route is called Partridgeville Road, which follows the southern side of the relatively wide and handsome Otter Creek, one of the area's top trout streams, eventually taking you to footpaths and snowmobile trails leading to Pine and Big Otter lakes on the Wild Forest's eastern boundary. Steam Mill Road quickly forks left from the southern route, the North South Road. Steam Mill Road hugs the Wild Forest's southern boundary, while allowing you to reach Pine Creek and, if you like a little bushwhacking, Little Pine Lake, just outside the Wild Forest's boundary.

In addition to being a center for logging, Brantingham Lake also attracted "sports" who came here to hunt and fish. The Child's Gazetteer of 1872 reported, "Brantingham Lake is a beautiful sheet of water irregular in shape and is entirely surrounded by forest which is full of game. The lake is well stocked with fish, pike, pickerel, and bass, pickerel being caught weighing three pounds."

A landmark of the area was Brantingham Lake Hotel, which catered to hunters and fishermen. In the early 1870s the hotel was almost destroyed by fire. What remained was sold to George Graves, rebuilt, and later called Brantingham Inn.

With the coming of the automobile, the resort business in the Brantingham Lake area declined. In 1966, the inn was torn down and the land was turned into thirty-one cottage lots. In 1984, a new inn, the Brantingham Inn Motel, was constructed to serve a new breed of recreationists—

snowmobilers, cross-country skiers, hikers, and drivers of all-terrain vehicles—as well as those who still come back to hunt and fish.

A railroad line, the Glenfield and Eastern, was built as late as 1928 to transport pulp and logs from the Brantingham Lake region to a huge band mill in Glenfield. Today a part of the railroad right-of-way, minus ties and rails, is still used, but now by snowmobilers and skiers in winter and hikers and ATV drivers in summer. It is known locally as the Glenfield Railroad Trail, serving as a quiet reminder of the area's logging past. Gone, too, are the sawmills and bark mills that once dotted this area; only a foundation is left here or an outline there, if you know where to look.

By the 1950s, the bulk of the land now making up Independence River Wild Forest had been acquired by the state and the forest was left to reclaim the land. Most of the area is covered by young forests, but the forest immediately east of Brantingham Lake is thick and tall. You need take only a few steps from the community surrounding Brantingham Lake to plunge into what has all the trappings of a remote, unpopulated wilderness. You can most easily experience this kind of environment if you take Steam Mill Road east.

Steam Mill Road—Brantingham Lake to Pine Lake

One of the principal routes into the southeastern section of the Independence River Wild Forest is Steam Mill Road, which begins just south of Brantingham Lake community. From here, Steam Mill Road runs in an easterly direction on a relatively straight course over level terrain to its terminus at a turnaround and parking area called the Drunkard Creek Trailhead.

To get to the start of Steam Mill Road, follow Brantingham Road to the first intersection west of Brantingham Lake. At this intersection, the road running north is called Van Arnum Road; the one running south has the tricky name of North South Road. Turn onto North South Road and drive south for 0.6 mile to the intersection with Steam Mill Road which begins as a two-lane hard-top road. It runs east for 2 miles past a golf course and a pond to the beginning of the Wild Forest, where it becomes a single-lane dirt track.

Several trails radiate from this road. The first is found 0.3 mile from the Wild Forest Boundary, where you will find a turnout and trail register.

This is the trailhead for the old Steam Mill-Pine Lake Trail, which has been shortened and converted into a cross-country ski loop. The second trailhead is found at the end of the road where the Pico Mountain Trail leads to Spring Hill Junction and a number of connecting trails for day hiking or backpacking.

78 Steam Mill Road Trail

Dirt road, driving, snowmobiling, walking, skiing, birding
3.4 miles, relatively level

Steam Mill Road can either be driven or hiked. In summer, well-shaded by a canopy of tall trees, the road is delightful and cool to hike. It is not plowed in winter; DEC has officially designated it as a snowmobile route. It makes a good ski trail, although you have to share it with snowmobilers.

The forest is open with a lush understory of ferns. Expect to see deer, owls, and a variety of warblers and vireos along the way. At the 1-mile mark, the forest parts to reveal open marshes on the right and just a glimpse of Fish Creek flowing through them. At 1.1 miles you cross the small wooden bridge over Poison Creek, which flows south a short distance to feed into Fish Creek. The smooth stone outcrop just west of the bridge tells a quick story of the glaciation that scoured the area more than 12,000 years ago. A large beaver meadow, with low vegetation and no trees, is found on the left.

At 2.6 miles you cross Fish Creek, which contains good-sized brown trout, and shortly beyond another of its feeder streams. At 3 miles you reach Emerson Creek. South of the bridge a short distance, but out of sight, are two small ponds surrounded by a swampy area.

The next gentle hill is a watershed divide. Land to the east drains into Drunkard Creek, which you meet at 3.4 miles, just beyond the road barrier at the trailhead.

79 Steam Mill Ski Loop—Pine Lake Trail

Hiking, cross-country skiing
6.2-mile loop, 3 hours, relatively level

From the parking turnout and trail register, 0.3 miles along Steam Mill Road from the Forest Preserve boundary, a trail used to run east for 5.4

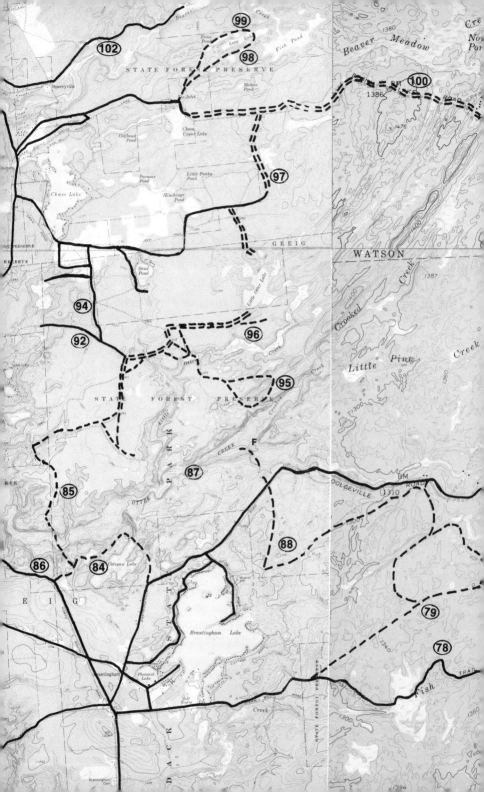

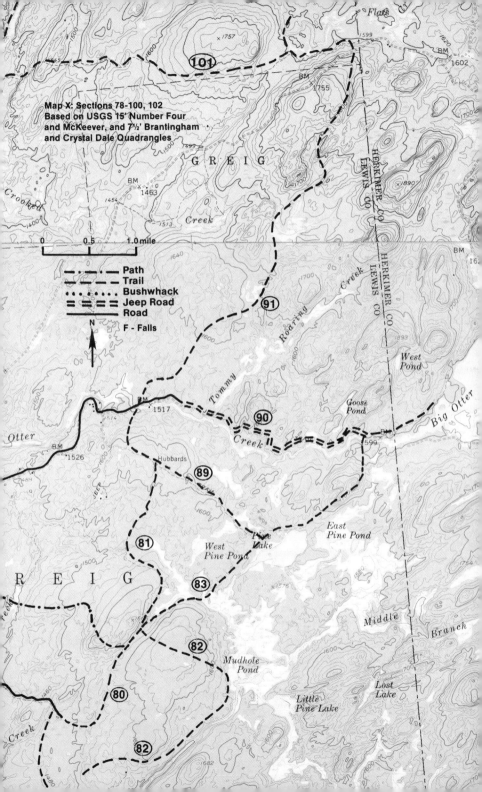

Map X: Sections 78-100, 102
Based on USGS 15' Number Four
and McKeever, and 7½' Brantingham
and Crystal Dale Quadrangles

0   0.5   1.0 mile

Path
Trail
Bushwhack
Jeep Road
Road

N

F - Falls

miles to the junction called Spring Hill. The 1986 DEC Unit Management Plan for the area calls for the closing of the eastern portion of the trail and the creation of a ski loop on the western end with a leg running off the northern portion to the Partridgeville Road in the north. The loop will be approximately 6.2 miles from Steam Mill Road over 4.5 miles of trail, with Partridgeville Road about 3 miles distant via either portion of the loop. The loop from Partridgeville Road will be approximately 4.5 miles long, and when completed, it will provide a good ski route through gently rolling terrain and tall forests.

As it is now designed, the trail will follow the old red-marked Steam Mill-Pine Lake Trail northeast for 1.7 miles to a new loop, which heads north for about 0.5 mile, and then loops sharply westward on high ground overlooking a small stream that flows westward and feeds into Brantingham Lake. At the 2.5-mile mark, the ski trail swings southwest for another 1.5 mile. About 0.5 mile from the starting point, it rejoins the old Steam Mill-Pine Lake Trail.

With map and compass and some bushwhacking experience, you can still walk the 2.5-mile eastern half of the old red-marked trail to reach Spring Mill Junction. This part of the trail, which has received little use for years and will no longer be cleared, has become weed-filled and more or less obliterated; but there are still long sections where the old trail can easily be distinguished.

Once you have covered the eastern 2 miles of trail, continue east. Soon you come to a low, marshy area where beaver appear active. Within another mile, you come to the headwaters of Fish Creek. Once across the creek, you begin a gradual ascent; about a mile from the creek, the ascent begins to become more pronounced as you start up the western slope of what locals call Big Pico Mountain—actually a hill with a vertical ascent of only 160 feet. Down the other side of Big Pico, the descent is sharp, bringing you to a low area where Spring Hill Junction is found and from where several other trails radiate, sections 80 through 82.

80 Pico Mountain Trail to Spring Hill Junction

Foot trail, former snowmobile trail, level walking, streams
1.8 miles, 1 hour, relatively level

From the Drunkard Creek Trailhead at the end of Steam Mill Road, you enter the woods on a wide, yellow-marked trail and cross a small wooden bridge over Drunkard Creek to the Pico Mountain Trail.

Crooked Creek

Immediately after crossing Drunkard Creek, you encounter another virtually unused trail forking right; this is the old Pine Creek Loop Trail which has been earmarked by the DEC to be closed, though the guideboard still indicates that it is 3.2 miles to The Mudhole on Pine Creek via this route. With map and compass, you can still hike this trail even though the pathway is weedy and in some parts hardly recognizable. It intersects the continuation of the still used portion of the Pine Creek Loop, section 82.

The abandoned trail heads south from Drunkard Creek for a short distance then starts to loop eastward, staying close to the Wild Forest southern border until it meets Pine Creek. It then follows Pine Creek on its west side in a northeasterly direction for 1.5 miles to The Mudhole.

The Pico Mountain Trail is your main route to Spring Hill Junction. It is a level walk through a thick forest of hardwood, mostly maples, stands that are indistinguishable from the Wilderness area to the east. This trail, too, starts off by heading in a southeasterly direction from the trail junction and register for a short distance to cross a small brook feeding into Drunkard Creek.

The trail follows the brook in a northeasterly direction. At 1 mile from the trailhead, the trail crosses this feeder stream again. You may be scarcely aware that the land is rising as it enters a cut between two hills. From the last stream, it is 1 mile over level ground and through thick woods to a junction known by several local names: Spring Hill (on the DEC map), Five Corners, and, for reasons which are not clear, Eight-foot Swamp Junction.

Whatever the proper name, the junction sits in a depression between two hills. In this flat land, however, any hill looks worthy of attention and deserving of a proper name. Just north of the junction is what people hereabouts call Big Pico Mountain and to the southwest is Little Pico Mountain. Their height may qualify them as hills, but to call them mountains seems to be stretching things a bit. Perhaps after walking for hours on level ground an early hiker found the sudden encounter with any land form impressive, and with a little imagination, a mountain was born from the 160-foot tall hills from which the trail takes its name.

At the junction you will find signs directing you to the various trails radiating from this spot, so you should have no difficulty selecting the route you want. The junction is the meeting of the abandoned portion of the Steam Mill-Pine Lake Trail, see above; the red trail that continues on to Pine Lake, section 82; the Pine Creek Loop Trail, which leads to The Mudhole; and this, the Pico Mountain Trail, which continues north.

81 Spring Hill Junction to Pine Lake Trail

Snowmobile trail, connector

2.5 miles, 1¼ hour, relatively level

This connector heads north from Spring Hill Junction, circles Big Pico Mountain on the southwest and then straightens out as it crosses a small stream and continues north to intersect the yellow-marked Pico Mountain Trail. Because it does not lead to any destination or shorten any hiking route, it has relatively little value for the hiker.

82 Pine Creek Loop Trail

Foot trail, abandoned snowmobile trail

1.4 miles one way, less than 1 hour, relatively level

This former snowmobile trail is the third route radiating from Spring Hill Junction. It is now a yellow-marked foot trail called the Pine Creek Loop Trail and it takes you to what is unglamorously called The Mudhole. It is no longer technically a loop as the portion back to the Drunkard Creek Trailhead, section 80, is to be abandoned. A short distance to the south is Little Pine Lake in the Ha-de-ron-dah Wilderness, which can be reached by bushwhacking on higher ground to the south of The Mudhole.

Much of the area east and south of The Mudhole is open and swampy as a result of several factors: the land is low; beaver activity keeps the water dammed up; and the "big burn" of 1909 destroyed hundreds of acres of forest east of the Mudhole and Little Pine Lake, giving the area its open appearance. It is a fairly attractive spot, typical of the swamps and marshes that interrupt the Adirondack forest.

To reach the area, follow the Pine Creek Loop Trail from Spring Hill Junction over the top of Little Pico Mountain in a southeasterly direction until you reach Pine Creek and the western tip of The Mudhole. In fact, The Mudhole looks like a thin, elongated lake, running from west to east, giving the impression that it is the headwaters of Pine Creek. This is not the case, for Pine Creek flows into this body of water on the north side. On the east side, it receives waters from streams flowing from Little Pine Lake in the south and Middle Branch Lake, Cedar Pond, and Middle Settlement Lake several miles to the east.

The Mudhole is a favorite spot for fishermen, some of whom bring in inflatable boats to use to catch the sizeable brook trout that inhabit this fingerlike body of water. There is a spot on the western tip of The Mudhole (and the continuation of Fish Creek) where boats can be launched, and according to last reports, two aluminum boats had been left there for use by fishermen.

83 Spring Hill Junction to Pine Lake

Hiking path, thick woods, some open areas
2.3 miles, 1½ hours, relatively level

From Spring Hill Junction, the so-called Red Trail, marked with red disks, heads off in a northeasterly direction following the contour line of the lower slope of Little Pico Mountain while staying on high ground overlooking a mile-long stream feeding into Pine Creek.

At 1 mile, the Red Trail approaches the crossing over this stream and makes a short, gradual descent to the stream. The area on the east side of the trail is open and swampy. This area, too, is part of the region devastated by the "big burn" of 1909. With beaver ponds keeping the area swampy, the forest has not been able to recapture the land.

Once over the feeder stream and past the swampy area, the Red Trail reenters the woods, staying well to the east of Pine Creek, but following its route. About 0.9 mile from the feeder stream crossing, you catch a glimpse through the trees of the southwest corner of Pine Lake. You continue northeast for 0.8 mile, following the shoreline of the lake, which is attractive, but typically Adirondack: trees come to the lake edge; there is no beach, just low growth that extends into the water. Shaped like a huge drop of water, the half-mile-long lake comes to a point on the west side and bulges round on the east. In summer the lake glistens a deep blue with its cool color enhanced by the deep green forest surrounding it. There is a lean-to at the north end of the lake.

A short distance to the east of Pine Lake and flowing into it lies its cousin, East Pine Lake. Between these two lakes, both of which are located in the Ha-de-ron-dah Wilderness Area, runs the Blue Trail coming from Middle Settlement lake, several miles east. This Blue Trail crosses into the Wild Forest and intersects the Red Trail a short distance north of the lean-to.

The Red Trail, which stays in the Wild Forest, follows that area's boundary in a northeasterly direction for 1.5 miles to where it intersects the Big Otter Lake Road at the western point of Big Otter Lake. Here, too, you find another Blue Trail, this one marked along the abandoned road that leads through the Wilderness Area to the Village of Thendara, 6 miles to the east.

If you add the Pine Creek Loop to a walk from the Drunkard Creek Trailhead, your total hiking distance from the start on Steam Mill Road (where the unplowed road begins) to the Pine Lake lean-to is 8.9 miles.

Partridgeville Road Trails — Brantingham Lake to Big Otter Lake

Another route into the hinterlands of the Independence River Wild Forest is by Partridgeville Road—a two-lane dirt road whose 7.5-mile length serves a number of snowmobile and foot trails to Catspaw Lake, Pitcher Pond, Shingle Mills Falls, Pine Lake, and Big Otter Lake.

Partridgeville Road is called Dolgeville Road on some maps, the latter name coming from Dolgeville near the Mohawk Valley, where Alfred Dolge had a large piano factory. He lumbered tracts in the Independence River area for cherry and other hardwoods, which were used for piano sounding boards.

Partridgeville Road branches from Brantingham Road, just west of the community surrounding Brantingham Lake. From the junction, Partridgeville Road runs north to bend around the upper portion of Brantingham Lake and then heads east along the south side of Otter Creek. En route the road cuts through a corner of the Wild Forest (in which is found the trail to Catspaw Lake), moves through a piece of private land, and then returns to the Wild Forest. The next 2 miles of road are located on state land, but then the road passes through a second private inholding, this one quite large, crossing it for 2.5 miles before again returning to state land.

Once you have reentered the Wild Forest, a short distance brings you to a bridge over Otter Creek; the road ends 0.5 miles from the bridge. From that point east, the road is reduced to a jeep trail with a name change; it is now called Big Otter Lake Road, which, if driven at all, must be traveled with a four-wheel-drive vehicle, since the jeep trail is narrow and rutted. It is really better to walk this portion of the trail; an easy 2.3 miles brings you to the western tip of Big Otter Lake.

Big Otter Lake Road follows the north side of Otter Creek, a well-stocked trout stream attracting anglers throughout the spring and summer seasons. En route to Big Otter Lake, you cross three streams feeding Otter Creek from the north, the biggest one of which is called Tommy Roaring Creek. All these streams contain trout, mostly browns with some native brookies.

Just north of Brantingham and Catspaw lakes, the sandy region begins, and as you continue northward, it also becomes a region of glacially produced ponds. The plains themselves are the product also of the glacial period, made by such rivers as the Otter and Independence, which were swollen by glacial waters as they carried sand downhill from the central Adirondacks.

84 Catspaw Lake—Catspaw Lake Road to Van Arnum Road

One-lane trail, easy walk
1.9 miles, 1 hour, gentle hills

Catspaw Lake has a number of floating bog masses at its northern end and beautiful forested shores to attract the hiker. A short portion of this trail takes you directly to it, or you can walk the whole trail for an extended outing.

At the intersection of Brantingham and Partridgeville roads, make a left turn and head northeast on Partridgeville Road for 1 mile. Here the road bends to the right and heads east. At the bend you also find a jeep trail (now extensively used by ATVs in summer and snowmobiles in winter) forking to the left; this is the beginning of the Catspaw Lake Trail. Park here and walk north.

The trail is sheltered by a tall canopy of hardwoods; the terrain is a series of small glacial hillocks, a contrast with the flat plains further south. Tall stands of hemlock shelter the deep slopes of what appear to be glacial ridges. The road bends to the left at 0.3 mile and heads downhill, reaching the outlet of Catspaw Lake at 0.8 mile, after only a fifteen-minute walk. A pine-covered knoll overlooks a sizeable beaver dam that has raised the level of the lake, freeing the bogs at the opposite end. These are not visible from the outlet, but if you follow the irregular shoreline around the lake's southern side, you can spot them.

The trail continues in a northerly direction; a little over 0.1 mile brings you to a bridge crossing the lake's outlet, which flows north then west to empty into Otter Creek. A short distance beyond, the outlet brings you to a trail forking to the right and heading north; this is Blueberry Trail, section 88, a snowmobile trail that runs along the south side of Otter Creek and loops back to Partridgeville Road.

The Catspaw Lake Trail bends left past the intersection and continues in a southwesterly direction for 0.5 mile where a second snowmobile trail forks right. This one has been given the somewhat out-of-place name, Erie Canal Trail, and it crosses Otter Creek and heads north, section 85.

Beyond this point, Catspaw Lake Trail turns sharply south. A gentle but steady uphill climb through deep forest brings you in 0.5 mile to the intersection with a one-lane dirt road, Van Arnum Road (unmarked). Here you have several options. You can turn north on Van Arnum Road, section 86. A walk or drive of 2.5 miles along it brings you to Otter Creek with its series of attractive step-falls, used by campers and locals for tubing down the shots and over the smooth rocks. On both sides of the stream are designated camp sites. Camping permits must be obtained from the regional office of the DEC in Lowville.

Another option is to turn south on Van Arnum Road, which in a mile brings you to the intersection with the black-top Brantingham Road. Follow Brantingham Road for 0.3 mile to the intersection with Partridgeville Road. Turn north on it and walk along it for 1 mile to your car.

Your third choice is to retrace your steps on Catspaw Road back to the Erie Canal Trail, which you can use to get to Pitcher Pond, section 85.

85 Erie Canal Trail to Pitcher Pond

Attractive foot trail, sandy roads, Pitcher Pond and its eskers
5.8 miles round trip, 3½ to 4 hours, relatively level

Van Arnum Road begins at the intersection with Brantingham Road, just about 0.5 miles west of the community surrounding Brantingham Lake. Drive along it for 0.7 mile to the entrance to the Otter Creek State Forest. Catspaw Lake Road is a right fork, just inside the boundary of the forest. From Van Arnum Road, your walk is about 0.5 mile on the Catspaw Lake Trail to the intersection with the Erie Canal Trail, section 84. At the intersection a sign indicates that Chase Lake is 3.6 miles to the north. Follow the Erie Canal Trail downhill to a narrow wooden bridge crossing the wide and fast-running Otter Creek, a bridge that is closed to all vehicles except snowmobiles. On the other side you start a gradual uphill climb along a wide walking path for about 0.5 mile before reaching level ground.

The trail is well canopied, making it a fine summer hiking trail. Once you reach the level section, another 0.5 mile walk brings you to a short gradual descent to a road junction, 1.8 miles from the start, with a well-used dirt road, McCann Road (unmarked), which runs in a southwesterly direction, and a narrow single-lane road forking to the right. There are several signs here, giving you directions back to Catspaw Lake, or further to Eatonville and Chase Lake. These are not the directions you want to go. Instead, turn to the right and head east on the one-lane dirt road called the Short Cut Road (unmarked). You reach another fork in 0.3 mile. The left leg is a grassed-over, little-used route called Nothing Road which in a short distance turns into Pitcher Pond Road. Short Cut Road, on the other hand, forks to the right and heads southeast for 0.3 mile to intersect Pitcher Pond Road.

As you walk along Short Cut Road, notice how the vegetation and soil change. The forest quickly gives way to open fieldlike areas covered with low-growing spirea and a scattering of aspens, cherry, and small pines; the soil, in turn, has become sandy. You have reached the Wild Forest's sand plains, the distinctive ecological zone that occupies the middle third of the region.

Once on Pitcher Pond Road, the trail swings due east and continues on the level sandy land for 0.5 mile to reenter a forested area and start downhill. As it nears the bottom, the road turns left and heads north about 0.2 mile. Through the trees on your right you can see Pitcher Pond. Suddenly you are aware that you are walking on what appears to be a circular dike, with the sides sloping sharply downward, on the right to the pond and on the left to a low, swampy area. This strange land form is an esker, but how the waters running under the glacier could produce an esker in the shape of a nearly complete circle is even stranger.

The circular esker forms a bowl containing the waters of Pitcher Pond which are fifteen feet higher than Little Otter Creek. A slight depression on the eastern side allows the pond waters to flow into Little Otter Creek, which flows in a semicircle around the northern and eastern sides of the pond.

The waters of the pond are murky and brown. Vegetation growing out from shore into the pond forms a spongy mass around the edge, creating what will one day become a bog.

The road stops on the west side of the pond. From there a herd path leads a quarter of the way around the pond almost to the outlet before it stops. Little Otter Creek flows south through a cut, fifty feet deep, made by the stream.

You can retrace your steps back to your vehicle on Van Arnum Road via Pitcher Pond and Short Cut roads and the Erie Canal Trail.

86 Van Arnum Road to Otter Creek Campground

Sandy roads, swimming, sightseeing
3 miles one way, 2 hours, 330-foot descent

Van Arnum Road is a sandy track running northward from Brantingham Road into a relatively small (1206-acre) piece of state real estate, Otter Creek State Forest. This state forest butts against the Independence River Wild Forest so that there is no distinguishable line separating the state forest from the Wild Forest.

Pitcher Pond

You can walk or drive to the turnoff leading to the state camping area and the bridge over Otter Creek where you have a nice view of the series of falls arranged in steps. The road is tree-lined and covered to give a cool, shaded walk. The way is relatively level, though varied with sandy hillocks, gullies, and low open areas—good places for birding and berrying.

The road descends the escarpment from 1250 feet to Otter Creek at 930 feet elevation. For those who like level terrain but varying scenery, this can be a delightful walk.

From Brantingham Road it is 0.7 mile to the entrance of the Otter Creek State Forest. Catspaw Lake Road is a right fork, so stay left. The route takes you outside the Adirondack Park. Forests of pine give way to hardwoods, aspens, birches, cherry, and maples, as the road angles in a more westerly direction. The terrain changes, too, becoming more rolling and irregular. The road remains nearly a half mile south of Otter Creek until near the end of Van Arnum Road. It is 2.3 miles from the entrance to the State Forest to an intersection where Van Arnum Road follows the left leg. The unnamed right leg is a jeep trail that touches Otter Creek.

Van Arnum Road now enters sand country, the plains left by the retreating glacier and glacial outwash. Here, along Van Arnum Road, the sands frequently appear in the form of dunes. In part the exposure of the sand resulted when the land was cleared for agriculture which was soon abandoned as winds removed the topsoil, leaving behind depleted sandy subsoils. Fire also eliminated the vegetation. What you see today is nature's slow efforts to repair some of the damage done by farmers and loggers.

If you take the jeep trail to the right, you will again find tall trees shading the road. In 0.4 mile, the jeep trail, which is close to Otter Creek, comes to a rise and passes under power lines. The opening gives a good view of the countryside with Otter Creek to the north and the rolling terrain to the south where the escarpment begins pitching downhill toward the Black River Valley.

A short distance beyond, the jeep trail intersects a dirt road, McCann Road (unmarked), on the right. You are now entering the camping area with designated campsites located just off McCann Road. A few hundred yards down McCann Road brings you to the bridge over Otter Creek. On summer days swimmers will be sliding or tubing down the smooth rocks that make up the falls.

Across the bridge, the road forks. McCann Road follows the right leg and heads east. If you follow this single-lane dirt road, it will take you in about 2.5 miles to Pitcher Pond Road. The left fork is unnamed and runs north, paralleling the creek, and reaching Nortenville Road in 0.8 miles. This loops back to McCann Road and the bridge.

87 Shingle Mill Falls and the Blueberry Trail

Good hiking, one of the best waterfalls on Otter Creek, fishing, photographing
4.5-mile loop, 2 hours, relatively level

From Brantingham Road it is 2.6 miles along Partridgeville Road to the point where Shingle Mill Falls Road, a single-lane, narrow track, heads north. You have to watch your vehicle's odometer since the entrance to the road is not all that obvious. Park on the north side of Partridgeville Road for the short walk to Shingle Mill Falls.

If you continue driving east for 0.1 mile, you reach the trailhead for the Blueberry Trail which intersects the Shingle Mill Falls Road, so you can start either place. A historical marker, 0.2 mile down Partridgeville Road, indicates a spring used by settlers since 1874. And in the next 0.2 mile, two paths lead to fishing spots along the Independence, which is here quite close to the road.

Starting north to walk along the Shingle Mill Falls Road, you come to a junction in 0.2 mile with the snowmobile route, Blueberry Trail, crossing the falls road.

Continue on Shingle Mill Falls Road for another 0.2 mile; a short descent brings you out to flat rocks that lead to the middle of the three falls. This portion of the walk takes no more than fifteen minutes. Its photographic opportunities make it an impressive destination. A path leads downstream below the lower falls for a fine view of all three cascades. The falls were the site of a matchbox and match factory and later the site of a sizeable mill in which shingles were manufactured.

If you are looking for more of a walk, retrace your steps and turn right on the Blueberry Trail. You can follow it as it roughly parallels Otter Creek where the creek turns to a southwestern direction. While the trail generally stays to the south of the creek, it approaches its banks several times before the trail ends at the Catspaw Lake Trail, just north of that lake.

The terrain is level at first, but gradually becomes marked with hillocks and dips. At the 1-mile mark, the trail overlooks the river from a vantage 120 feet above it; the river appears to be virtually straight down below. The trail continues along this edge for 0.7 mile as it turns southward to reach the Catspaw Lake Trail in another 0.3 mile. The trail passes through a heavily wooded area, a beautiful mix of hardwoods and evergreens.

At the intersection, you have several choices. You can retrace your steps via the Blueberry Trail or you can complete a loop by taking Catspaw Lake Road to Partridgeville Road and then back to your parked vehicle.

88　Glenfield Road Trail
Old railroad right-of-way, snowmobile trail
3.6 miles, 2 hours, relatively level

From the entrance to Shingle Mill Falls Road, section 87, it is only 0.1 mile on Partridgeville Road to DEC signs on both sides of the road. On the left is the trailhead to Blueberry Trail with signs indicating 2.3 miles to Catspaw Lake and 6.5 miles to Chase Lake. On the right, south, side of the road, the DEC sign reads "10-mile Crossing 3.5 miles." This is the Glenfield Railroad Trail, and it follows for the most part the roadbed of what was once the railroad line of the Glenfield and Eastern, a company that operated into the late 1920s, transporting logs and pulp wood from the Brantingham Lake area to a mill in Glenfield. The old roadbed and the name "Glenfield," however, are all that remain of the bygone logging era.

The trail runs south from Partridgeville Road and loops back, northeast along the right-of-way to reemerge at 3.6 miles at Partridgeville Road, 2.2 miles east of the starting point. The 2-mile section on the right-of-way is now just a smooth, level path. You can use this to tie in with the Steam Mill Ski Loop or walk back along Partridgeville Road, making a 5.8-mile circuit.

89　Pine Lake Trail to Pine Lake
Hiking path, lean-to, camping, fishing
2.8 miles, 1½ hours, relatively level

Continue by car east on Partridgeville Road for 4 miles beyond the Blueberry Trail intersection to a bridge over Otter Creek. Just before the road reaches the bridge, you encounter a parking area on the right (south) side of the road. The trailhead of the Pine Lake Trail is found here. En route, this road passes through a 3-mile section of private lands with cottages and hunting lodges on both sides. You reenter the Forest Preserve 0.2 miles west of the trailhead.

Across the road from the trailhead, you will find an unmarked footpath made by fishermen; it follows the south side of the creek. To get a good view and a nice feel for this most attractive trout stream, you can try walking a short distance on this footpath before taking off on the Pine Lake Trail.

The Pine Lake Trail, marked with yellow disks, runs over level ground and through a thick forest made up predominantly of hardwoods. It heads south for little over 0.5 mile, then takes on a southeasterly direction. At 0.8 mile, you come to an intersection with a snowmobile trail coming from the south: this is the Pico Mountain Trail (see section 81).

Up to this point the trail has been climbing ever so gradually; it now proceeds on a level area for almost 1 mile before making a hardly noticeable descent to Pine Lake. At 2.4 miles, the Pine Lake Trail bends fairly noticeably to the left and heads northeast for about 0.2 mile and then swings due south for a short distance to intersect the Red Trail, section 83. When you come to the Red Trail, turn left, northeast, and follow a footpath now marked with red disks along the Pine Lake shoreline a short distance to a path coming in on the left. This path runs a few hundred feet to high ground where you will find a lean-to. The area around the lean-to is open enough to allow several tents to be pitched.

Back on the Red Trail, if you continue northeast on it for a little over 0.1 mile, you will encounter another footpath intersecting on the right. At this point, you are standing on the boundary separating the Independence River Wild Forest from the Ha-de-ron-dah Wilderness. The right fork, marked blue, heads into that Wilderness. The Red Trail continues to Big Otter Lake. The ideal day hike is a loop that starts at the Pine Lake Trailhead on Partridgeville Road, goes to Pine Lake, follows the Red Trail to Big Otter Lake, and returns to the starting point via Big Otter Lake Road. For the Big Otter portion of this 6.5-mile loop, see section 90. You can turn this hike into a weekend adventure with a stay at the lean-to. Pine Lake contains brook trout, brown bullheads, white suckers, and sunfish.

90 Big Otter Lake Road to Big Otter Lake

Camping, trout streams, swimming, fishing
3.6 miles, 2 hours, level one-lane road

The principal route to Big Otter Lake is this jeep road, which is not suitable for driving for most vehicles. Most of the road is torn up by wheels, making it less than desirable as a hiking route. When the road reaches the western tip of Big Otter Lake, it turns northeast, following the lake's shoreline for 1.5 miles. This section of road is being closed to vehicular travel, making it a hiking-only route. The road, however, can be used as access to the lake and as part of hiking loops to Pine Lake, section 89.

To use the Big Otter Lake Road as a trail to the lake, leave your car in the parking area on the west side of the Otter Creek Bridge, which serves as the trailhead for the Pine Lake Trail. Cross the bridge on foot and continue on the dirt road for a little under 0.3 mile to a small, square parcel of private land containing several buildings that serve as a hunting lodge. Continue on the road past the buildings (and posted signs) into the wooded area, reentering the Wild Forest. The road now narrows and begins to have water-filled ruts.

From here on, Big Otter Road is a one-lane, rutted jeep trail. You cross five feeder streams flowing south into Otter Creek. You reach the first and largest of these streams after 1 mile; it is Tommy Roaring Creek, which holds naturally reproducing brown trout. The next three streams are unnamed, but one receives its water from Goose Pond, a small body of water 0.5 mile to the north. The last, just past the proposed vehicle barrier, gets its water from West Pond, which lies a mile north in the hill country that encircles the lake. Just beyond you reach the intersection with the Blue Trail to Thendara and the Red Trail to Pine Lake. And just beyond is the western tip of the lake.

Big Otter Lake is shaped roughly like a wedge, coming to a point at its western end. It is two miles long and half a mile wide at the northeastern end. You can walk along the lake's western shoreline for 1.5 miles to the site of an old hotel. This part of the road, which has recently been barred to vehicular traffic, is apt to be wet and rutted, and the ruts will probably last for years. The lake's eastern shoreline is the boundary with the Ha-de-ron-dah Wilderness. As a result, no motor boats are permitted on the lake, but float planes do still fly fishermen in.

Tree-lined and sparkling, Big Otter Lake is a most attractive body of water. It is a reasonably good fishing lake, containing brook trout along with bullheads and sunfish. It is a good lake for swimming, and you might enjoy an inflatable boat to explore the shoreline.

91 Silvermine Trail to Balsam Flats and Independence River

Snowmobile trail, open beaver meadows, and balsam
7.2 miles, 3 hours, relatively level

The third trail radiating from the parking area at the beginning of Big Otter Lake Road has the curious name Silvermine Trail. Around the turn of the century fly-by-night prospectors and other local hopefuls were searching for natural resources that might bring them wealth. Some small amount of minerals were found, including iron ore. There was actually enough ore to start a mining and smelting operation in the Port Leyden area. It did not last long because of the impurities in the ore, but it existed long enough to whet the appetite and stimulate the imagination of those who saw sudden wealth in discovering rich materials.

Local legend has it that searches were made for silver in the belief that the area contained a vein or two. The talk was long and the hope great, but nothing was found. Still, the name "Silvermine" and its fuzzy legend has remained, officially attached to a snowmobile trail running from the end of Partridgeville Road to Independence River in the north.

The Silvermine Trail runs a distance of 5.6 miles to a junction with Balsam Flats Road and Mount Tom Road. The latter is a little-used jeep trail. Another mile eastward on the extension of the Mount Tom Road brings you to a fork; the right (northern) leg of which takes you in 0.6 mile to a bridge over the Independence River.

The terminus of the Silvermine Trail is on the southern edge of a fairly large area called Balsam Flats, an area that lives up to its name by being flat as a table top and covered with a stand that is predominantly balsam. A north-south boundary line passes through Balsam Flats so that the western half falls into the Wild Forest and the eastern half lies in the Webb property, and, hence, in private hands where logging continues.

The Silvermine Trail is typical of the southern half of the Independence Wild Forest. It is a deep woods trail, level and running a relatively straight course with few outstanding natural landmarks. The terrain's flatness makes it an easy trail to hike and the thick forest, which provides welcome shade during hot, sunny days, provides a surrounding with its own charm. The trail gives you a feeling of remoteness, and, although outside an officially designated Wilderness area, it provides a route for walking through an untamed wilderness, a good trail for a backcountry weekend camping trip.

To find the start of the trail, just walk east from the parking area at the end of Partridgeville Road, across the bridge over Otter Creek; a few steps more brings you to the trailhead on the right, north, side of the road.

The beginning of the path is wide, but during the summer months it is grass- and weed-covered, though late-summer trailwork in preparation for the snowmobile season keeps the trail clear.

The trail leaves Partridgeville Road, heading in a generally northeasterly direction, with a rise so gentle (100 feet) between 0.5 and 1.5 miles that it is hardly noticeable. In this section you pass three small ponds on the east side of the trail; they are set back so far they go unnoticed unless you make an effort to search them out.

At the 3-mile mark, however, you come to a vast open beaver meadow through which flows Crooked Creek and one of its larger feeder streams. The headwaters of these streams lie in swamps a mile to the east. Crooked Creek flows southwesterly into the beaver meadow, then loops north for 0.3 mile, crossing Silvermine Trail, before it eventually straightens out to run a westerly course toward Otter Creek. You cross the creek on a wooden bridge at 3.2 miles, a short distance to the north of your first sighting of the beaver meadow.

Beyond, the trail gradually bends to the right, heading in a more easterly direction through a low-lying area; 0.3 mile brings you to a second bridge, this one over the feeder stream. The trail stays on the south side of the feeder stream for the next 0.3 mile, where it turns somewhat sharply left at 3.8 miles, heading north to cross the feeder stream a second time.

Now the trail begins to rise in a noticeable way, and in less than 0.5 mile you climb 140 vertical feet—not much to be sure, but in this flat country, you will be aware of this ascent.

From the last bridge over the feeder stream, it is a straight path north northeast for 1.4 miles to a road barrier on a section of the trail called Harris Road. You reach a second road barrier and the end of Mount Tom Road, section 101, coming in from the west 0.4 mile farther on Harris Road, which is the width of a snowmobile trail.

The Independence River meanders calmly through the flatland 0.2 mile to the northeast. The section north of the junction is heavily wooded with mixed stands of hardwood as well as spruce, pine, and balsam fir. From here it takes a bushwhack to reach the river, but if you head west on the one-lane, rutted dirt road, Mount Tom Road, section 101, for a little over a mile, you will encounter a fork. Mount Tom Road continues as the left leg; the right leg is a snowmobile trail that takes you to the bridge over the Independence River, now racing swiftly westward. Once over the river, the snowmobile trail turns west to parallel the river for almost 1 mile before turning north; this portion of the trail on the north side of the river is known as the East Bridge Trail and it leads to several routes connecting with the Number Four-Stillwater roads, sections 113 and 114.

The distance from Partridgeville Road to the bridge over the Independence is 7.2 miles; only the levelness of the route makes this a possible 14.4-mile round trip for the average hiker. A weekend camping trip will make the distance appear shorter and allow you time to do some exploring or make the connection with the northern trails.

Chase Lake Area

COMPARED WITH THE thick forests to the north and south, the Chase Lake area is a world apart. The lands look as if a part of the African veldt had been transported to this part of New York. You need only a giraffe to emerge from the surrounding brush to complete the picture.

While this vision may be the product of too fertile an imagination, the unusual vegetation does much to inspire it. Physiographically, the terrain is dully flat; ecologically, it is covered with lichens and mosses and low-growth spirea, meadow-sweet—acres and acres of it—mixed with spotty growth of small trees, aspen, cherry, and Scotch pine. Long winters, short growing seasons, and pockets where frost persists to make even shorter seasons combine to inhibit plant growth.

All around you there is sand, miles and miles of it, made most conspicuous by the network of roads that have laid bare the sandy soil. This maze of jeep roads and trail may be the region's most distinctive feature—a mind-boggling network of crisscrossing, intersecting, and interlocking pathways, which, if you don't have a good topographical map and a handy compass, can get you turned around and hopelessly lost.

All this, of course, sets this portion of the Independence River Wild Forest apart from the northern region, with its rolling and stony but forest-covered terrain, or the southern region, with its tall trees and wet lowlands. Yet amid all the area's openness and flatness are found ponds and lakes of varying size, all located in a small, 12-square-mile area.

This is a land of many names—sand country, plain country, lake country, ATV country, and snowmobile country. But for many more who like to do their traveling on foot, it is also hiking and skiing country, and both these activities are growing in the region. For those who fear the tortuous roots and rocks, the occasional seas of mud, and the unsure footing of so many Adirondack trails, this is the place to walk or ski.

This is also a land of unusual road names bestowed by travelers with either a sense of humor or a sense of frustration. These include Brooklyn Square Road, Elbow Road, Proceeding Road, Dragline Road, Bull Road, Blue Jog Road, Confusion Flats Road, Erie Canal Road, Extra Road, Nothing Road, and to round things out, Useless Road.

The area has a short, uneven history of farming. The sand flats in the Chase Lake area were originally farmed by Hungarian immigrants, many of whom have descendants living in the Black River valley in and around

Greig and Glenfield. Evidence of this early farming can be found in old furrows that are still visible in some of the open fields.

However, when these settlers cleared the land for crop fields, much of the thin topsoil was swept away by wind, exposing the sand below. As a result, many of these early farmers turned to lumbering. But before logging became fully established, the fires of the early 1900s took their toll.

The pioneering plants, spirea and shadbush, are home to much wildlife. Ruffed grouse eat the meadow-sweet buds, and deer and rabbits eat its twigs. The shadbush, or serviceberry, attracts flocks of cedar waxwings as well as raccoons, squirrels, and chipmunks. Scatterings of black cherry, pin cherry, aspen, and pines dot the shrub-filled fields.

Chase Lake, at a mile in length, is the largest body of water in this central region, and is wholly privately owned. Many homes are clustered tightly around its shores and in the hamlet of Sperryville immediately north of the lake. There are also summer homes around the small Sand Pond, located 1.5 miles southeast of Chase Lake. The rest of the area is state land.

Two different routes bring you to the area surrounding Chase Lake. If you come from the north via Lowville and the hamlet of Watson, 3 miles east of Lowville, take River Road, a county highway running south from Watson on the east side of the Black River to intersect Chase Lake Road. Driving 5 miles east on that road brings you to the intersection with another blacktop road, Erie Canal Road. However, 0.5 mile before reaching this intersection, Chase Lake Road changes its name to Brooklyn Square Road, which takes you in 1 mile to a cluster of homes that constitutes Sperryville.

If you turn right, south, onto Erie Canal Road, you will cross a high bridge over the Independence River and at the mile mark you cross the outlet stream of Chase Lake. Here, three roads run to the left, east; two of them lead to the community around Chase Lake.

A second route to Chase Lake is via Pine Grove Road from the hamlet of Greig on the east side of the Black River. Three miles north of Greig, the road crosses Otter Creek and then forks. A sign directs you to take the right, east, fork. This blacktop highway, called Chases (note spelling) Lake Road, brings you to Chase Lake from the south. En route you drive through the full width of the 1453-acre Independence River State Forest, which is outside the Adirondack Park and butts the western boundary of the Wild Forest. You will need a good road map to sort out its route. It intersects Chase (note spelling) Lake Road-Brooklyn Square Road coming from the west, where north-running Chases Lake Road changes its name to become Erie Canal Road as it continues northward.

A number of roads and trails branch in an easterly direction from the Chases Lake-Erie Canal Road artery. It is convenient to divide the area reached by these access roads into two parts—one north and one south of Chase Lake. Three access routes take you into the southern section: Hiawatha Road, Lewis 35 Trail, and Sand Pond Road. Three roads take you into the northern part: Stony Lake Road, Bailey Pond Road, and Beach Mill Road. The latter leads to Payne Lake and Cleveland Lake via Cleveland Lake Road.

Chases Lake Road Route—To the South and Southwest of Chase Lake

Approaching from the south, Hiawatha Road and Lewis 35 Trail are the first two routes you encounter. Both are single-lane dirt roads, used by snowmobiles in winter and ATVs in summer. The former is officially classified by the DEC as a jeep and snowmobile trail, the latter only a snowmobile trail. Both, though short, can be hiked. They take you into an area just as easily reached by Sand Pond Road and Confusion Flats Road. They are included as hiking trails because they allow you to see the sudden transition from the forest ecology to the plains.

Sand Pond Road, a two-lane, hard-surfaced dirt road, is the more direct route if you use your car. It gives access to the Chase Lake sand plain via Confusion Flats Road, which is the most direct access to such scenic spots as Little Otter Creek and Lake and Crooked Creek Falls.

92 Hiawatha Road Trail to Confusion Flats Road

Thick woods, level trail, sand plain
1.4 miles, ½ hour, level

Turn off Pine Grove Road north from Greig onto Chases Lake Road. The second road intersecting on the right, 2.5 miles northeast, is Hiawatha Road, unmarked except by signs that designate it as a snowmobile trail leading to Chase Lake and Sand Pond and others that indicate the names of private homes to the south of the road.

About 0.8 mile down Hiawatha Road through a thick forest you come to a fork. The more traveled route goes right, immediately entering private land and continuing to two small ponds with summer homes. You turn left, north, onto the designated jeep and snowmobile trail. The walking is easy and, with the canopy of trees overhead, also pleasant.

The route is gradually downhill. A little less than 1 mile from the fork you see an abrupt change in environment: the forest is behind you and the spirea-covered sand plain lies ahead. Here also you intersect a single-lane sand road, Confusion Flats Road (unmarked). Hiawatha Road ends here and Confusion Flats Road takes over, bending right and running east. Within a mile, five other roads radiate from Confusion Flats Road, providing you with your first hint as to why the route is so named. You can continue on; the connecting routes are explored as extensions of the Sand Pond Road, sections 93 through 96.

93 Lewis 35 Trail and Blue Jog Road to Confusion Flats Road

Short snowmobile connector, level route, open vistas
1 mile, ½ hour, level

Why so many short roads carry a wealth of strange names is difficult to understand. That this short section should have the odd designation Lewis 35 Trail on its western half and Blue Jog Road in the east is especially odd. It is a level, single-lane dirt road, designated as both a snowmobile and a jeep trail. The ATVs that ply it keep the trail's grass cover worn down in summer. The trail is intersected on the north by Tip Road and ends at the north-south Confusion Flats Road. It, too, makes the transition from thick hardwood stands to spirea- and lichen-covered fields. Unless you are looking for exercise, there are shorter routes to the Confusion Flats area.

94 Sand Pond Road to Confusion Flats Intersection

Open fields, sandy roads

The two-lane dirt road called Sand Pond Road runs east from Chases Lake Road about 0.8 mile north of Lewis 35 Trail. Nearby, a state historical marker tells that 54,000 acres were burned here in 1913, after earlier fires in 1903 and 1908. The wide road bends to the right to swing around the southern part of Chase Lake. The first road branching from it is Tip Road,

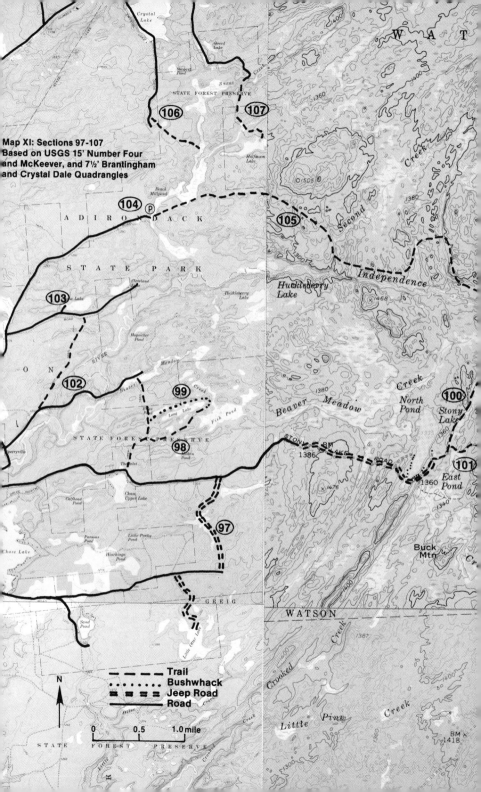

Map XI: Sections 97-107
Based on USGS 15' Number Four
and McKeever, and 7½' Brantingham
and Crystal Dale Quadrangles

Trail
Bushwhack
Jeep Road
Road

N

0   0.5   1.0 mile

and the second at 0.7 mile is Confusion Flats Road, which you can drive with a car. You will encounter some deep water-filled ruts on this road, and when you do, after 0.5 mile or so, you may wish to park and start walking south.

As you travel south you find open land covered with spirea and spotty growth of aspen and cherry trees. The openness makes the area appear friendly, a place where you might like to take time out to tent and bird. On the other hand, it is a strange land with the sandy soil covered thickly with springy mats of lichen.

Two roads angle in from the right 0.3 miles south of Sand Pond Road; one is just another route from Sand Pond Road and the other is Blue Jog Road coming from the west, section 93. Two more roads intersect 0.5 mile farther on, this time on the left. One comes from Sand Pond, a private inholding; the other, running southeasterly, is Eight Road (unmarked).

It soon becomes clear that this area has a bewildering maze of roads and why this part of the plain is aptly named Confusion Flats. A first-time visitor should not wander about these roads without the appropriate topographic map, the USGS 7.5-minute Brantingham quadrangle. Even such a map, though showing the roads, does not provide names for them. To make matters really challenging, your journey through the area is on unmarked roads, so this is a good place to practice using map and compass.

At 0.8 mile south on Eight Road from Sand Pond Road, you encounter Hiawatha Road coming in from the right. Confusion Flats Road now bends to the right and continues in a southwesterly direction for 0.3 mile. Here it meets Pitcher Pond Road coming from the south. At this point, 1.8 miles from Sand Pond Road, Confusion Flats Road turns southwest toward the Park Boundary. You now are in the area called Confusion Flats, where several roads converge. One of them is called Florence Pond Road; it moves off to the east to a low area in the spirea-covered land where ATVs have ranged over the sand banks.

95 Confusion Flats to Crooked Creek Falls

Fishing, hiking, birding
3.5-mile loop, 2 hours, relatively level

At the intersection with the south-running Confusion Flats Road, Florence Road heads east over level, spirea-covered land for 0.2 mile where it enters a low area, a depression shaped like a shallow saucer. At this point, too, a short (0.4 mile) road, Extra Road, heads south. Needless to say, the

Road in the Barren Sand Flats

names mean nothing since there are no identifying signs and some of the segments are remarkably similar.

The land to the south and east begins to change, for here forest is recapturing the sand plain. But while the sand plain has ended, the confusion of roads has not. Some of the confusion can be minimized by staying on Florence Road, following it eastward from Confusion Flats Road through the low area and over a gully into the forest. From the entrance into the forest it is less than 0.2 mile to a fork. The left leg is the continuation of Florence Road; the right is a narrow lane, Grownin Road (unmarked), which runs in a southeasterly direction for a little over 0.2 mile to a bridge over Little Otter Creek. As Grownin Road nears the creek, it bends to the left and runs due east along the north side of Little Otter Creek. It intersects Bank Road coming from the north and then bends sharply right to a bridge over the creek.

Beyond the creek crossing, the trail climbs a small grade back into woods and continues south. In 0.3 mile you come to a grassy trail formerly designated for snowmobiles. It intersects from the left; you can use this as the return segment of the loop trail. The land opens up again in fields of spirea, and 0.5 mile past the creek, the trail swings left, reentering the woods again. The terrain continues level as you travel east, then northeast for a little less than 0.5 mile where the other end of the loop forks left.

Go right and begin climbing a small hill. After 0.2 miles, the trail forks again. The right leg takes you down a fairly steep descent for 0.25 mile to Crooked Creek. Return to the main trail and continue over the low hill and down the other side; at this point you will see water gleaming through the trees on your left. This is small, narrow Long Pond, not to be confused with a larger Long Pond to the north. No paths lead to it and the trail passes well to the south of it.

If you continue on for 0.3 mile, you reach a foot trail forking right that leads in another 0.3 mile to Crooked Creek. Here there is a drop in the stream producing a small but attractive falls, a delightful place to picnic. Even though the segment north of Little Otter Creek is a designated jeep road, driving this far to shorten the trip is not recommended.

96 Little Otter Lake

Swimming, fishing
1.9 miles, 1¼ hour, relatively level

Follow the course outlined above as far as Bank Road and turn north on it for 0.3 mile to its intersection with Little Otter Creek Road (unmarked), which runs east for 0.7 mile through some open land and then through a wooded area to a fork. The right leg takes you in about 0.5 mile to a low area bordering Little Otter Creek. The left leg takes you in 0.3 mile to the south shore of Little Otter Lake.

Two footpaths, close together, lead a short distance from the snowmobile trail to the lake's edge. The second brings you to a nice sandy beach. If no one is fishing here, you can plan on taking a dip; the water is clear and delightful. The lake is completely surrounded by woods. Across the lake to the north is a private dock that serves the owner of a small portion of the north end of the lake. The rest is public property.

ATVs and other vehicles find their way here, for fishermen enjoy the lake's brown and rainbow trout as well as bullheads.

To return to your vehicle, follow Little Otter Creek Road westward from the lake to Bank Road. Continue west past Bank Road for 0.2 mile to a second intersection, Florence Road, coming in from the south. Turn onto Florence Road and follow it for 0.5 mile until it takes a southwesterly direction into a low area with the gully you crossed earlier. Another 0.2 mile in a westerly direction brings you back to Confusion Flats Road.

97 Hinchings Pond Trail

Open fields, jeep and snowmobile trail
2.5 miles, 1 hour, level

Another of the area's connector roads, open in the west to vehicles and for its entire length to snowmobiles, has limited value as a hiking route since the one attraction on its route is on private property. Sand Pond Road continues east and ends at the second of two dirt tracks that head south to private property around that pond. Here the route becomes a single-lane road with a new name, Hinchings Pond Road, which changes its name to Hinchings Pond Trail after 1.3 miles. As the road reenters state land, it reaches a junction where Bull Road heads south to private land, another road curves north and west to private land, while the narrow lane of the Hinchings Pond Trail continues straight ahead.

This trail runs east through forested land for 0.5 mile and then turns north, staying on the east side of a small unnamed stream for 0.7 mile. At this point it crosses a small beaver meadow and a stream and reenters the woods. The trail joins Stony Lake Road 0.5 mile beyond.

Chase Lake Road-Erie Canal Road Route — To the North and Northeast of Chase Lake

A half mile north of Sand Pond Road on Chases Lake Road you reach a tight cluster of three roads running to the east. The first is a dirt track that takes you in less than 0.5 mile to the Chase Lake Resort and Lodge, a private establishment that controls access to the western portion of the lake. By paying a fee, you can use the beach for swimming; you can also rent boats and sailing crafts there.

The second road, called Lake Shore Drive North, leads to private property around the lake. The third east-running road is Stony Lake Road, a two-lane, hard-surfaced road. It is a long route that leads you deep into the eastern interior of the Wild Forest. This eastward-bound route includes 5.5 miles of Stony Lake Road (which continues eastward as Mount Tom Road) with a spur, Fish Trail, running northward to the Independence River. The 4.5-mile-long Mount Tom Road passes through a 2-mile-wide private inholding en route to Balsam Flats on the Wild Forest's eastern boundary. You can drive Stony Lake Road as far as Chase Upper Lake, but the eastern portion of the road becomes a rutted jeep trail, making it for most people a hiking route. This makes the Stony Lake Road access to the eastern portion of the Wild Forest a very long one, since the one-way distance is 7.5 miles. If you include the spur route, Fish Trail, to the Independence as part of your hiking agenda, the distance increases to 10.5 miles. Round-trip travel, obviously, takes two days, so you may want to use this route as part of a weekend camping expedition and choose an alternate leg, sections 91 and 105.

98 Stony Lake Road to Fish Pond

Hiking, skiing
0.9 mile, ½ hour, level

Stony Lake Road leads first through private lands, then the Wild Forest, returning at 1.8 miles to private land surrounding attractive Chase Upper Lake. This small, angular lake is encircled by hardwoods and evergreens. Summer cottages snuggle in the pines around the northern end, but the southern shores are state-owned.

Stony Lake Road passes over a small channel of water connecting Chase Upper Lake with a small pond located immediately to the north. Just beyond this point, a single lane track heads north, left. The track, called Evies Pond Road, snakes northward, climbing to high ground. In 0.3 miles it reaches the end of private land, and shortly beyond there is a fork to the right.

This right fork is a little-used lane that runs a fairly straight and level course through deep forest. Three small round bogs are located immediately north of the trail, a short walk from it. Huge white pines grace the trail's end. While the route is one of the more pleasant walking trails in the area, the destination may prove a disappointment. Fish Pond was created by an old dam that has recently washed away, leaving a large mud flat peppered with stumps and snags. Perhaps beaver will repair it in the future and restore the pond to its former 0.5-mile length with four tiny islands.

Fish Pond is really part of Beaver Meadow Creek, which begins 3 miles to the east in a large wetland area and empties into the Independence River. The trail ends at the western tip of Fish Pond. Search along the northern side of the trail to find a small footpath along which you can make a short trip north to Long Pond, section 99. You can also use this path to make a loop walk.

99 Evies and Long Ponds

Camping, nature walk
0.2 mile, level

Drive 0.5 mile north on Evies Pond Road from Upper Chase Lake to where the road bends west and a second lane forks right. There is barely room for a car to park off the road here. Walk east along a low esker that continues as the high ground between two ponds, both of which are bogs, with sedges and sphagnum dominant. Both have little outflow of water and are filling with vegetation.

Fish Pond

An attractive campsite caps the esker above the western end of Long Pond. A narrow footpath threads the esker along the north shore of the pond, and turns south around its eastern end to lead to Fish Pond, reaching that pond near its outlet. That walk adds about 0.5 mile of hiking. If you make a loop from the better parking area at the fork for Fish Pond, you will have a delightful and varied 2.1-mile hike.

100 Mount Tom Road to Fish Trail and the Independence River

Hiking, camping
4.7 miles, 2½ hours, relatively level

To reach this road, you must either have a four-wheeled vehicle or be prepared to walk most of the 2.5-mile eastern portion of Stony Lake Road to the private inholding surrounding the lake. The jeep trail takes you to the southernmost tip of the lake. Beyond this point the road assumes a new name, Mount Tom Road, and after bending around the lake's southern tip, follows the lake's eastern shore. In just over 0.5 mile it reaches a north fork. The right leg is the continuation of the Mount Tom Road;

the left leg is called the Fish Trail, which begins at the road barrier. You are still on private land at the fork, but 0.2 mile north on Fish Trail you reenter state land. The state will construct a new parking area in this vicinity, so in the future you may be able to start your walk here, shortening the trip to about 1.5 miles if the road is also improved.

The west side of the Fish Trail is bordered with low, flat land, which becomes swampy as the trail nears the river. The east side is bordered with a ridge of low hills ending in a circular hill, Mount Tom, 200 feet above the surrounding area, which in this flat country makes it a prominent land form.

The trail splits just before reaching the river. The right leg, the continuation of Fish Trail, takes you to a road barrier. Past the barrier, the trail leads in 0.3 mile to a narrow foot bridge that allows you to get to the river's north side with dry feet. The left leg takes you to the river's edge. When the water is low, you have a ford that drivers (mostly hunters) of four-wheel-drive vehicles cross with ease. You can wade across under low-water conditions if you don't mind wet feet. When the water is high, it's a different story; all travel halts on the south side of the river.

Once across the Independence ford, you meet a spur trail running west to become a yellow-marked hiking trail called the Beach Mill Trail, which takes you westward across Third Creek to Gleasmans Falls and eventually to Beach Millpond Trail, section 105. If you cross on the footbridge you can continue your hike on Fish Trail which runs for 0.4 mile along the northern side of the Independence and then turns north, following the west side of Fourth Creek and eventually leading to Panther Pond, section 108.

101 Mount Tom Road to Balsam Flats

Winding trail, hilly terrain
4.8 miles, 2½ hours, 400-foot elevation change

From the intersection with Fish Trail, Mount Tom Road runs eastward to terminate at Balsam Flats. This rutted jeep trail passes through a large private inholding that shows evidence of intensive logging done over the years. Although the state has obtained an easement to allow public use of the road, barriers have been erected at the east and west boundaries to prevent unauthorized vehicles from using the road. "Unauthorized" means

Evies Pond

everyone except the private landowners and their guests. The road can be walked, though, since the easement restricts traffic to foot travel.

As Mount Tom Road winds eastward, it gradually gains 400 feet in elevation as it winds and dips and climbs over a series of small hills. As soon as Mount Tom Road leaves the private inholding by Stony Lake and enters state land, it crosses a small south-flowing stream and then starts climbing the first of three small hills. The dips between the hills are low and, after a rain, wet.

The route over the first hill is relatively steep, requiring a climb of 145 feet in 0.2 mile. The trail then dips and crosses a stream, reaching a barrier at 1.2 miles at the beginning of the private inholding. The second hill is not quite as high or as steep; the climb is 80 feet. When the trail comes to the third hill, it makes its highest climb—a long and gradual 157-foot ascent. As the trail starts downhill, at 3.2 miles, it leaves the private inholding and passes the second barrier. The descent is a bit steeper than the ascent. As it nears the bottom of the hill, at 3.8 miles, the trail intersects a snowmobile trail, called the East Bridge Trail, which forks north from Mount Tom Road. A short distance northward, this trail crosses a snowmobile bridge over the Independence River, turns west along the river's northern side, and then turns north again to intersect Panther Pond snowmobile loop, section 114.

Mount Tom Road continues eastward, staying on the south side of the meandering and twisting Independence River, which is here moving slowly through flatland. In under a mile it reaches the junction with Balsam Flats Road, the jeep trail coming from the southwest, and the Silvermine Trail, a snowmobile route also coming from the south. The junction is a short distance south of a forested flat area called Balsam Flats, section 91.

102 Brooklyn Square-Bailey Road Route to the Independence River

Spirea-covered fields, sand dunes, slow river, fishing
1.8-mile road from Sperryville

Traveling north on blacktop Chases Lake Road from the intersection with Stony Lake Road brings you in 1.5 miles to a junction. Chase (note spelling) Road comes from the west; just before reaching the junction it changes to Brooklyn Square Road. Chases (note spelling) Lake Road, on which you are driving, ends at the junction, becoming Erie Canal Road as it continues north from the junction.

Turn right, east, onto Brooklyn Square Road and drive 0.8 mile to Sper-ryville with its small cluster of homes. Here Brooklyn Square Road ends and Bailey Road begins, becoming a single-lane dirt road as you travel east. You can drive or walk along the next 1.8 miles of Bailey Road. You pass a spirea-covered field on the left and an exposed sandy area over which ATVs are run. The Independence River, slow-moving here and tree-lined, lies south of the road. The river twists and turns its way through this area and is most scenic—well worth a stop. It has cut a trough through the sandy soil down to resistant bedrock; smoothed boulders now protrude from the river like the backs of hippopotamuses.

Fishermen also seek out the Independence for it contains trout. Unhap-pily, acid rain has affected the river and reduced the fish population a bit.

Traveling northeast on Bailey Road brings you in 0.3 mile to a spot where the Independence River almost touches the road on the right; the sharp drop to the river is 50 feet. In 0.2 mile you come to the first intersection on Bailey Road—this one with Proceeding Road (unmarked), a short link closed to vehicles but open to hiking.

Just beyond, and also on the left, is a jeep trail heading north over the sandy, spirea-filled landscape. This jeep trail, which serves as a snowmo-bile trail in winter and an ATV trail in summer, is called Old Number Four Road (unmarked). It is a good hiking route, running in a relatively straight line northeast for 0.7 mile to intersect Cleveland Lake Road, which can take a hiker to Payne Lake to the west or Cleveland Lake to the east. For more detailed descriptions of these routes, see section 103.

Old Number Four Road runs over quite lumpy terrain, although the hil-locks are small. The beginning and end of this trail are through fields but the trail's central section is tree-covered. About midway, you come to a spot where a loop of the Independence River swings westward to within 200 feet of the trail. A short walk will bring you down a slope to river's edge.

Just beyond Old Number Four Road, another road forks from Bailey Road. This right fork runs a short distance to the northern edge of the Independen-dence. Here's where locals come to swim, fish, and tent. You are now en-tering an area in which the Independence twists and turns, even splits around an island. It is a low, flat country through which the river meanders leisurely. Canoeists who like flat water will enjoy this part of the river.

By continuing eastward 0.2 mile on Bailey Road you reach a left, north, fork that also leads to the river and at 0.6 mile you reach a bridge over the Independence which is here flowing north to south. Here, too, is where Beaver Meadow Creek empties into the Independence. The river is here a wide and handsome waterway with trees sitting back from the bank. The river's width and openness make it a good fly-fishing stream and with a little luck and skill, you might land enough brook trout for supper.

The road continues a short distance beyond the bridge, but it now enters posted private land, so you have to turn about and return to your vehicle.

103 Beach Mill Road to Payne Lake

Road, fishing, swimming, camping
1.4 miles from Erie Canal Road, 1 hour, relatively level

The first road to intersect Erie Canal Road a little more than 0.5 mile north of Brooklyn Square Road is Beach Mill Road, a single-lane dirt road running east. The cover here, primarily pine, is thick on both sides of the road and continues for the next 0.4 mile. Beach Mill crosses another dirt road, McPhilmy Road, which runs a southeasterly course to Sperryville.

At the 0.4-mile mark, spirea fields appear on the right and stretch to the south along the eastern flank of McPhilmy Road. A short distance farther, 0.4 mile, you will encounter a little-used road running south 0.3 mile to intersect McPhilmy Road. At this point the land opens on the left to the same spirea-covered landscape, and continues so until you reach Cleveland Lake Road (unmarked) forking to the right at about the 1.1-mile mark. Just before the fork, the road again enters forest land.

You can either walk or drive to this intersection with Cleveland Lake Road, but if you drive, you ought to park at the intersection and walk the rest of the way. The road, while well used, is a level, single-lane route that is pleasant to walk. Trees, mostly hardwoods, on both sides of the road arch over the trail and shade you in your eastward travel.

A walk of a little over 0.5 mile brings you to a fork. The left leg runs down a gradual slope through a cathedral of tall pines to Payne Lake, a clean, sparkling, and attractive lake 0.3 mile long and a little over 0.1 mile wide. From Cleveland Lake Road it is about 0.1 mile to a small, sandy, tree-shaded beach where people come to fish, swim, and tent. This lake has been cleaned of trash fish and restocked by the DEC with brook trout, and that is all the lake contains. Payne Lake and its immediate environs make up one of the most attractive and accessible spots in the Independence River Wild Forest.

A close second in attractiveness is Cleveland Lake, but it lies entirely within private land and is therefore off-limits. Nonetheless, Cleveland Lake's scenic qualities make it worthwhile to walk the road eastward for 1 mile to have a look. Cleveland Road runs straight east, paralleling Payne's southern shore. In a little less than 0.5 mile, you enter private property. At this point you find a narrow trail running north on the left side of the road. This snowmobile route, called Cleveland Lake Trail, crosses private land for 0.4 mile where it enters the state forest; in 0.5 mile more it intersects Beach Mill Road.

Cleveland Lake Road is a public thoroughfare, so you can cross the strip (0.4 mile wide) of private land to reenter the Wild Forest. The road now heads north and in 0.1 mile loops westward to a barrier on the eastern edge of Cleveland Lake. End your walk by turning around and heading west to your car.

104 Beach Mill Road to Trailhead and Beach Millpond Trail

Good road, site of old mill
2.2 miles from Cleveland Lake Road, 1 hour, level

From the intersection with Cleveland Lake Road, Beach Mill Road continues northeast then east, coming to an end at a parking area and the access point to the yellow-marked hiking route, Beach Millpond Trail, which takes you to Gleasmans Falls on the Independence River and beyond, section 105.

This single-lane road, running over hard-packed sand, is a fine route for automobile travel; and so you may want to drive to the trailhead. If you are looking for a good place to walk, you will find it runs over level land with hardly a rut. From the intersection with Cleveland Lake Road, it is 1.5 miles to where the land opens up to spirea-filled fields. Crossing this sandy terrain is a trail coming in from the south, Cleveland Lake Trail. Quickly the scene changes as you reenter a wooded area, and 0.3 mile further the scene changes to open fields. Here the fields are filling with aspens, cherries, maples, and beeches, a demonstration of natural succession in all its lustiness.

The road ends in a small parking area that overlooks a low area partially filled with water. This is the southern tip of Beach Millpond, a grassy flow that was once a pond nearly three-quarters of a mile long. You need walk only a few steps downhill to Burnt Creek, which beaver have dammed, thus restoring a portion of the pond. The site of the old mill, no longer visible, is on the south end of the pond.

105 Beach Millpond Trail to Gleasmans Falls and Beyond

Foot trail, waterfalls, fishing, camping
3 miles, 1½ hours, relatively level

Gleasmans Falls is one of the premier destinations in the region. It is an easy one-day walk, but continuations of the trail make it a delightful back-packing destination for those who wish to continue exploring the Independence River as far as Balsam Flats, combine it with a loop around Stony Pond, or connect with the trails on the north, sections 108 through 114.

Gleasmans Falls is one of the more attractive scenes along the river. Here you see a series of falls with water dropping more than sixty feet in about a quarter of a mile. As water rushes over the falls, it is squeezed at the bottom through a rock-lined flume or gorge, with sheer rock cliffs approaching seventy-five feet high. Above the falls, the stream is strewn with large boulders around which the water rushes on its way to the falls. Boulders below the falls give the river a wild, chaotic look and the noise of rushing water echoes through the valley. The Independence River is exercising its freedom and vigor; perhaps scenes like this inspired the river's name.

The falls is a nice place to be on a warm, sunny summer day, sitting on a smooth rock with feet dangling in the water. Bring lunch and stay awhile to enjoy the sights and sounds of this wild place. Other parts of this twenty-eight-mile waterway are flat and slow-moving as if the river, growing tired, were feeling its age. Here it tumbles and dances down rocky ledges like a young person, full of energy and excitement.

The Beach Millpond Trail is yellow-marked and generally level in its eastward course, crossing three streams. The first of these, Burnt Creek, is immediately east of the trailhead. From here it is 0.4 mile to where the trail comes within a stone's throw of the southern bulge of Beach Millpond; you can see the pond's water through the trees on your left. Another 0.8 mile brings you to small, narrow Nickel Creek.

Hiking through this forest is pleasant, primarily because the trees are so well spaced that the forest has an inviting, open look, allowing you to see long distances in all directions. The dominant hardwoods are maples. The trail gradually turns to the south and in another 1.5 miles over level terrain you reach a point where a gradual downward slope begins. It is hardly noticeable at first and continues southeast toward the Independence River.

Gleasmans Falls

Soon you come to two huge boulders next to the trail, erratics picked up far to the north by the glaciers in their advance 20,000 years ago. Beyond, the trail angles a little to the right and heads down a sharply pitched slope. At this point you hear and see the river at the same time, but paradoxically what you see is not a river but a boulder-strewn dry river bed. Where's the river you hear? It is on the other side of the heavily treed island that stands in front of you. Only during heavy spring run-off does it rise high enough to spill water around the north side of the island which then splits the river in two. All this becomes clearer as you continue eastward along the river's edge and come to the footbridge over a third small stream, Second Creek.

The trail now takes you through a pine stand, up a rise, and over rock outcrops. The sound of rushing and tumbling grows stronger; then you are looking at the series of step-falls, with a deep pool at their feet, and the flume. On the far side of the pool is the wall of a story-high boulder. Beyond it, the water picks up speed as it rushes down through the garden of boulders. This is what you have come to see, so stay awhile. It is primordial, and this is the charm and attraction at Gleasmans Falls.

If you are planning a camping expedition, you will have the time to continue eastward. The yellow-marked trail hugs the north side of the Independence River for 0.7 mile, then loops north and around the top part of a small, square parcel of private land. Here the trail crosses a wooden bridge over an unnamed creek flowing south to join Third Creek, just before the latter empties into the Independence River.

Once past this unnamed creek, the trail turns southward and in 0.5 mile reaches the bridge over Third Creek. A short distance beyond the bridge, Beach Millpond Trail intersects a spur trail coming from the Fish Trail, section 100. There is a barrier to prevent snowmobilers from turning onto the hiking trail. This marks the end of Beach Millpond Trail. Fish Trail can be taken south over the Independence 2 miles to Stony Creek or followed east almost a mile to the west bank of Fourth Creek. Fish Trail then turns north following Fourth Creek for 0.7 mile and, a short distance farther, crosses Snake Creek. A short distance farther north, Fish Trail meets the terminus of a yellow-marked trail coming south from Panther Pond, which lies a little over a mile to the north, section 114.

Along the Number Four-Stillwater-Big Moose Roads

THE SHAPE OF the northern region of the Independence River Wild Forest resembles a huge finger pointing eastward from a closed hand. On a map, roads that border the region on the north look like a long string from which hang three lakes: Crystal, a privately owned lake in the west, Lake Francis and Sunday Lake in the Wild Forest. These bodies of water act as major reference points since the access roads that take you into the northern region cluster close to them. Here, all the access roads run south from the major east-west two-lane roads and take you to a wide assortment of lakes, ponds, streams, beaver meadows, wetlands, and small hills.

From Crystal Lake in the west to the far end of Stillwater Reservoir in the east is 21 miles. In the region's western section, Number Four Road acts as a northern boundary and the Independence River is the southern boundary.

The access roads seem to characterize this region of the Wild Forest, but there are other more distinguishable characteristics. The soil becomes gradually deeper as you move to the east, and the terrain slopes upward, becoming hillier and more rugged. More stones and boulders are visible in the forest floor, with rock outcrops becoming common in the Panther Pond and Fourth Creek areas.

There are several things, however, that the northern region has in common with the lower half of the Wild Forest, things that are particularly important to the foot traveler: an extensive network of trails and an interesting combination of road trails, jeep trails, snowmobile trails, and officially designated hiking trails. There is enough variation in all these to make hiking here a unique and enjoyable experience.

The area's history of logging is similar to that of the southern part of the Wild Forest, as is its devastation by forest fires. An 1891 map of the "Great Forest" depicting the proposed Adirondack Park shows denuded and burned areas at Stillwater, Sunday Creek, Lake Francis, and Burnt Creek. The practice of "high-grading" conducted in the early logging days led to a preponderance of beech and a scarcity of hemlock still noticeable today. Just before the turn of the century, this area witnessed huge log and pulp drives. Logs cut in this area were floated down the Beaver River to one of the largest mills in New York State, located at Castorland by the confluence of the Beaver and Black rivers.

There were other less spectacular moneymaking activities in the area. Before logging overwhelmed the area, "pickers" searched the forest for spruce gum; a history of the area reports pickers in 1887 coming out of the forest carrying up to 100 pounds of gum. North country guides catered to "sports" who came to such favorite spots as the Number Four and Beaver Lake area in the north for fishing, hunting, and camping.

Men of wealth and influence were found here. Clarence Fisher, a well-known lumberman and landowner, held large tracts of land. He conveyed two large parcels to the state and recently his estate conveyed most of Francis Lake to the state.

William Seward Webb's name is still associated with a large tract of private land adjoining the Wild Forest's eastern boundary, and much of what is today's Wild Forest was originally Webb land. When a law in 1893 authorized the raising of the dam at Stillwater Reservoir, Webb filed a lawsuit claiming that the impoundment had isolated 66,000 acres of land, making them unavailable for logging. This suit led eventually to the largest acquisition of land for the Forest Preserve ever made: 47,326 acres from the Webb tract were obtained by the state in 1896.

The John Brown Tract was named after John Brown, who participated in the Revolutionary War, founded Brown University, and served as Governor of Rhode Island. Lake Francis was named after another Governor of Rhode Island, Brown's grandson, John Brown Francis.

Wildlife is abundant in the area, with large white-tailed deer wintering areas near Halfmoon Lake, Burnt Creek, and Sunday Lake. You may spot black bear, eastern coyote, beaver, muskrat, fisher, otter, mink, snowshoe hare, raccoon, and ruffed grouse.

The various streams, ponds, and lakes support a variety of fish and though the state does some stocking, the area's fisheries are supported mainly by native species, naturally reproducing.

The region, while relatively level and heavily forested, does have its own charm and eye appeal. The drive from Number Four to Stillwater Road is scenic any time of year, but especially in fall after the leaves turn. Perhaps nowhere in the Adirondack Park are so many scenes of water interspersed with forest and wetland as in this northern part of the Wild Forest. The largest assortment of wetlands with small areas of uplands is found in the Burnt, Second, Snake, and Sunday Creek areas and around Lizard Spring Brook. These wetlands are a vital resource since they provide open

areas in the solid forest cover as well as food and nesting sites for water-fowl and furbearers.

Forest cover varies from west to east. In the west, pioneering species are found, white pine and aspens with red spruce, balsam fir, and tamarack circling the ponds. As you move to the east you will find tall forests of northern hardwoods with mature pine crowning the ridges of gravelly gla-cial soil.

In the Sunday Creek-Lizard Spring Brook area are numerous small bogs, and several eskers are east of Sunday Creek. The network of trails takes you to many fishable streams.

Access to the region is along Number Four Road, which begins from the community of Watson, just east of Lowville. You will find a good mac-adam surface until you reach Stillwater Road, a two-lane dirt road. It can be a bumpy ride for the last 8 miles to Stillwater Reservoir. Just before the hamlet of Stillwater, a dirt road forks right and heads south. This por-tion is called the Big Moose Road. It, too, gives you a bumpy ride before the macadam surface returns. Much of the land bordering this road south to Big Moose Lake is privately owned. The road ends at Eagle Bay and NY 28, making this the principal access point for those coming from the east.

The roads heading south from this road system are all single-lane dirt tracks. Some have been resurfaced and graded; others have not. In any case, most of them should be driven only by four-wheel-drive vehicles even though in dry seasons, a passenger car can get you a good distance south on some of them. Many make good cross-country ski routes since they are not plowed in winter. This guide will treat them as hiking routes.

Number Four Road—Trails in the Northwestern Region

Three access roads run south from Number Four Road: Crystal Lake, Half-moon, and Smith roads. If you are driving east from Lowville, you come to the hamlet of Watson as soon as you cross the Black River. At the eastern edge of Watson, the road forks, with Number Four Road begin-ning with the left fork. At 6.5 miles you reach the crossroads of Crystal-dale. From Crystaldale it is 3 miles to the next crossroads and Crystal Lake Road heads south from it to take you to Burnt Creek. The next access road, just a short distance east from the Crystal Lake access road, is Halfmoon Road, which you can follow to Halfmoon Lake. The third access, Smith Road, is 3.5 miles east of Halfmoon Road, and it starts you toward Panther Pond and points south along the Independence River.

106 Crystal Lake Road to State Land and Burnt Creek

Easy walking, good fishing
2.5 miles, 1 hour, level

Burnt Creek holds brook trout, a species any dedicated fisherman is willing to travel far to catch. In planning your hike here, be sure to bring your fishing gear. If you would rather hike than fish, you will not be disappointed. The area south of Crystal Lake is a most pleasant one to explore.

Crystal Lake Road is a public thoroughfare running south from Number Four Road for 0.3 mile to cross Crystal Lake's outlet stream and continue for 0.4 mile along the lake's western shore before passing between two houses. The road continues south and in 0.3 mile, you will see on your left a state Forest Preserve marker. This is a good place to leave your vehicle and start walking. The road continues south along the boundary of state land for another 0.2 mile and then bends to the right, heading in a more southwesterly direction. Another 0.2 mile brings you to a fork the right leg of which is a private route running back to Number Four Road. The fork's left leg continues southwest for 0.2 mile to the intersection with the Burnt Creek Road snowmobile trail, which heads southeast into deeper forest. Take this trail south and you will notice that a short distance into the forest, the road begins to make a slight descent, a drop of thirty feet, and then levels out, only to gradually climb out of the shallow hollow. If you follow this hollow eastward for a short distance, it will take you to a small, unnamed bog pond.

Once the Burnt Creek Road trail comes out of the hollow, it continues its southeasterly course in a relatively straight line. The trail gradually descends fifty feet to Burnt Creek. From the intersection with Crystal Lake Road to Burnt Creek itself, the distance is 0.6 mile. Looking downstream, you can see the northern edge of Beach Millpond, section 104. Upstream there is a swampy area close to the creek, and even further upstream, the creek widens to become part of an extensive wetland which in wintertime serves as a deer yarding area. This important wetland starts just west of Halfmoon Road, section 107, and extends southward to include Beach Mill-

pond and the area adjoining the Independence River. The high ground overlooking the northern edge of Beach Millpond makes a good place to take a break and picnic. It is less than a mile back to your car from here.

Crystal Lake Road continues beyond the intersection with Burnt Creek Road for 0.3 mile to deadend at the Forest Preserve line. If you are adventurous and have a map and compass, you can bushwhack from the road's end in a southeasterly direction for 0.5 mile to the western shore of Beach Millpond.

107 Halfmoon Road to Halfmoon Lake

Hiking, cross-country skiing, swimming, fishing, camping, skiing
1 mile, ½ hour, level

Continue 0.7 mile east from Crystal Road along Number Four Road to the single-lane dirt track running south, Halfmoon Road. Although you can drive your car 1.5 miles to the first road barrier, this portion of the road is attractive enough to invite hiking. Of course, like all the dirt roads in the area, it is unplowed in winter, so then you would have to ski the entire length.

Level and well shaded, it runs due south for 0.5 mile through private land before crossing the northern boundary of the Wild Forest. Once inside the Wild Forest, it continues south through a predominantly hardwood forest for almost 0.5 mile where the road makes a sharp elbow turn to the left. In a short distance it crosses a small south-flowing brook. The water comes from a small pond, Gourd Lake, 0.2 mile north of the road. The road continues east in a straight line for a little less than 0.5 mile, then bends south and in 300 yards reaches a road barrier on the north side of Burnt Creek.

After crossing the wooden bridge over Burnt Creek, you make a gradual climb uphill for a short distance. The road now runs on level terrain and continues south for 0.7 mile to a second road barrier, which marked a private inholding acquired by the state in 1980. The buildings at the lake edge were removed in 1986.

The last barrier is on the north side of a small brook, and from here it is 0.3 mile to the eastern edge of Halfmoon Lake. Pines crown eskers that ring the lake; sheep laurel and wild cranberries ring the shore. The lake, which is widest in the east, tapers to a point in the west. It is 0.5 mile long and 0.1 mile wide and fits well with the image of an Adirondack

Halfmoon Lake

lake—clear, dark blue, with its shore lined with tall evergreens, mostly white pine.

The area on which buildings once stood is ideal for camping and the lake is inviting for swimming. Fishing is currently limited to sunfish and bullheads, but the state has plans to stock it with game fish.

You can camp where the buildings stood, or picnic there after a short hike or ski.

108 Smith Road to Panther Pond and the Independence River

Good road, snowmobile trail, hiking, cross-country skiing, lean-to
3.5 miles road, 4.4 miles trail, relatively level

Number Four Road intersects Smith Road 3.5 miles east of Halfmoon Road, section 107. You have the option of driving Smith Road to a barrier 3.5 miles southeast of Number Four Road or walking that distance. Smith Road has been repaired and graded and is well maintained to make vehicular travel safe. But the route, well shaded and level, is a delight to walk or ski. There is enough variation in the vegetation, terrain, and scenery to make it interesting as well. It is not plowed in winter.

In summer, if your plans call for reaching the Panther Pond lean-to, 1 mile south of the road barrier, or the Independence River, 2.5 miles from the barrier, you might wish to drive all or some part of Smith Road before taking off on foot for these places deep in the interior.

A DEC report calls the foot trail network around Panther Pond one of the most attractive in the region, but notes that the lean-to only gets occasional use—no more than 75 people a year—most of whom are fishermen and hunters. Hence, the Panther Pond area and the region south are worth a day's hiking, or better yet, a weekend visit.

Smith Road has a generally level track though it winds through terrain that has occasional hillocks and hollows. The route is heavily forested with breaks in the solid forest cover only around Panther Pond, along the upper reaches of Pine Creek and the lower end of Third Creek. White pine and hemlock mix with the predominantly hardwood forest.

Because the terrain slopes down from the northeast, the headwaters of several ponds can be found to the northeast of Panther Pond, among them Burnt, Pine, Third, and Hay creeks, all of which are crossed by the region's trails.

Just after Smith Road heads south from Number Four Road, a lane intersects on the right. This road runs a couple hundred feet to what used to be a fire ranger's house and, on high ground behind the house, to a fire tower. Both structures have been removed.

After heading south for almost a mile, Smith Road bends to the left and heads east for about 0.5 mile. You pass a gravel pit on the left. Although not visible from the road, Burnt Creek is a short distance south of Smith Road, which parallels the creek as it flows first north and then west.

At the gravel pit, the road bends to the right. It heads south and in 0.5 mile it reaches a fork. The road straight ahead is blocked by a road barrier to prevent people from entering a rectangular-shaped private inholding. Smith Road turns sharply to the left to follow the border of the inholding, heading east for 0.3 mile. It now turns right and heads southeast, shortly crossing Burnt Creek. The road continues in a southerly direction for another 0.5 mile where it intersects Panther Pond Loop, formerly designated as a snowmobile trail that headed south. A yellow-painted road barrier stops vehicular traffic from entering; maintenance of the trail will soon be discontinued.

At this point, Smith Road turns sharply to the east and in a little over 0.5 mile comes to a bright orange barrier on the north side of Pine Creek, a fair-sized stream at this point. This is where Smith Road ends. Across Pine Creek the trail narrows to become an officially designated foot and snowmobile trail.

Just west of the road barrier, a little-used, grass-covered trail forks to the left and runs in a northeasterly direction. The state has made no provision for the use of this old route, but at one time it took you to Bills Pond, headwaters of Burnt Creek. With topo map and compass, you can find your way along this old trail to the pond, which is a mile away.

Once past the barrier and across Pine Creek, you climb a small rise as the trail turns to the southwest. In 0.2 mile, you reach a junction from which three trails radiate. One, the continuation of the hiking trail you are on, is now called the Lean-to Spur; it runs southeast. Another is the snowmobile portion of the Panther Pond Loop that heads southeast. You will meet it when you hike to the Snake River. The third, called the North Crossover Trail, is a snowmobile trail heading east to McCarthy Road and is described in section 114.

For the present, stay on the Lean-to Spur as it travels southeast on high ground overlooking Pine Creek a short distance to the north. In 0.7 mile, the Lean-to Spur intersects a trail forking right. This short trail ties into the western portion of the Panther Pond Loop.

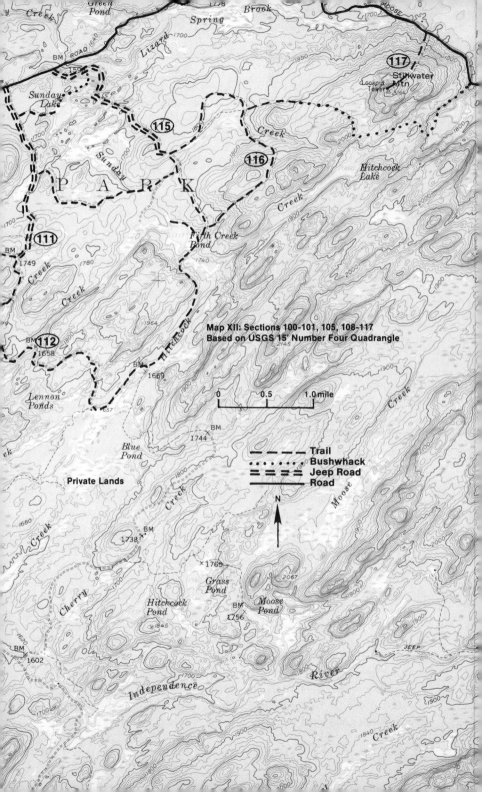

Map XII: Sections 100-101, 105, 108-117
Based on USGS 15' Number Four Quadrangle

117 Stillwater Mtn

115

116

111

112

Sunday Lake

Lizard

Spring Brook

Green Pond

Creek

Lookout Tower

Hitchcock Lake

Fifth Creek Pond

P A R K

Sunday

Creek

Private Lands

Lennon Ponds

Blue Pond

Cherry

Hitchcock Pond

Grass Pond

Moose Pond

Independence

Moose

River

Creek

Creek

0   0.5   1.0 mile

Trail
Bushwhack
Jeep Road
Road

N

After a short but gentle descent, you arrive at the Panther Pond lean-to, overlooking this attractive body of water surrounded with tall trees. The pond is fairly wide at its north end, the half-mile-long pond tapers to the south.

If you are on a weekend backpacking trip, the lean-to can give you shelter for a night's lodging. Even if you are only on a day hike, you should tarry at this spot for a picnic. The state has limed this lake to reduce its acidity and it is currently stocked with game fish.

A yellow-marked foot trail begins on the left side of the lean-to. It offers the best route south to the Independence River and beyond. It starts out by bending around the northeast end of Panther Pond before heading due south, paralleling the pond's eastern shoreline. About 0.8 mile south on this footpath, you cross the upper reaches of Third Creek into which Panther Pond outlet feeds a short distance to the west of the trail. Lying to the left of the trail is a large beaver meadow through which Third Creek flows. You can see the meadow, actually a swampy area, through the trees on your left.

Once over the Third Creek foot bridge, you climb a rise that suddenly gets a bit steep for a short distance before leveling out. As you continue south through the dense hardwood forest, the land becomes a little more rolling, although the hillocks and depressions are small.

A mile south from Third Creek, the Yellow Trail brings you to a low area on the north side of Snake Creek and an intersection with an old snowmobile trail that was part of the western half of Panther Pond Loop. This 3-mile trail, which leads back to Smith Road, could be an alternate route to this point but you will encounter low, wet areas as you move northwest along Snake Creek and where the trail crosses Third Creek. Plans call for maintenance to be discontinued on this portion of the trail.

Just after you cross Snake Creek, you encounter the eastern snowmobile-designated portion of the Panther Pond Loop, which heads east, left, at the intersection. The right fork, heading southwest, is the Fish Trail, section 100, which takes you to the bridge over the Independence River and beyond.

To follow Fish Trail to the river, head southwest. You soon pass a small open area on the left and what looks like a small pond. All this, however, is part of Fourth Creek, which has its headwaters about 8 miles to the east. By the time it reaches this pondlike impoundment, Fourth Creek is a fair-sized stream. The Fish Trail parallels the creek on the west side for almost 0.7 mile to the confluence with the Independence River. A new foot trail, not completed in 1986, is to be constructed heading east along the river for 1 mile. At the confluence you will find a huge white pine log stranded high above the river's waterline. It may have rested here since the log-driving days early in this century. The stranded log is about fifty inches in diameter, larger than almost all that are harvested today.

About 0.3 mile upstream from Fourth Creek, there is an eye-catching gorge on the Independence through which the water races for about 800 feet. This is the lovely section the new trail will follow. Pinxter bushes bloom in spring beneath stands of large, old-growth spruce and hemlock.

You now have several options. You can elect to return to Panther Pond and eventually to Smith Road by the same route you took to get to the confluence. Or you can lengthen your return by using the eastern Panther Pond Loop as far as the junction with the Lean-to Spur Trail.

A third option is to continue your trek south by following Fish Trail south over the Independence River to Mount Tom Road, just east of Stony Lake, and then east on Mount Tom Road to East Bridge Trail, which, in turn, you can follow north to the Independence River, sections 100 and 109. The distance of this route is 7.5 miles, and you would include it in your hiking plans only if you chose to camp for a second night.

109 Independence River to Smith Road via Panther Pond Loop

Hiking, backpacking, fishing
5.5 miles, 3 hours, relatively level

One way to return to Smith Road is by following Fish Trail from the Independence River north along the west side of Fourth Creek for 1 mile to the junction where Fish Trail converges with the Yellow Trail (coming from Panther Pond in the north) and Panther Pond Loop Trail from the east.

The DEC, however, is planning to construct a 1-mile section of trail running east from Fish Trail at the confluence of Fourth Creek and the Independence River to East Bridge Trail. This trail probably will be finished about 1990. It will allow you to walk a loop from Fish Trail via the new spur trail and East Bridge Trail to Panther Pond Loop. This new route covers a distance of 2.4 miles. Once on the Panther Pond Loop Trail, you can then continue north until you reach Smith Road.

In the meantime, you can pick up the eastern section of Panther Pond Loop Trail by hiking north from the Independence River on the Fish Trail to the junction. Here you turn right, east, onto the Panther Pond Loop, which runs eastward between Snake Creek in the north and Fourth Creek in the south.

The area along this route is heavily forested and flat. However, you will pass by or through some open sections—low, swampy areas in which beaver are active. The first low, wet area south of the trail is 0.6 mile north of the confluence of Fourth Creek and the Independence River; 0.8 mile more brings you to still another soggy section lying just south of the trail along the upper reaches of Fourth Creek. At the 1.7-mile mark, the loop trail enters a large beaver area and just as it does it meets the snowmobile route, East Bridge Trail, coming from the south.

The loop trail now swings around the northern edge of the marsh area as it continues eastward. In spring and after a heavy rain, this section of trail can become quite soggy, but soon the trail climbs onto higher, drier ground until it comes to the western side of Fifth Creek at the 2-mile mark. At the 3-mile mark it reaches the intersection with Emmett Hill Road, section 113, coming from McCarthy Road in the north. The junction is the corner of the Wild Forest boundary; to the east and south is private land. Immediately south of the junction is a section of Fifth Creek that has widened to give this body of water the look of an elongated pond.

The loop trail now turns left and winds its way over level terrain in a northwesterly direction. From the intersection, it is 2.5 miles to the Lean-to Spur Trail, the trail you walked on your way south. The loop trail here follows an old logging road that snakes back and forth, staying on fairly dry and level ground. It passes a small pond, and the headwaters of Third Creek are south of the trail near its midpoint.

When the loop trail reaches the Lean-to Spur Trail, it also reaches the junction with the North Crossover Trail from the east. You can turn right, north, onto the Lean-to Spur Trail, and 0.3 mile brings you to Pine Creek, the road barrier, and Smith Road.

Stillwater and Big Moose Roads—Trails in the Central and Northeastern Region

Stillwater Road, a two-lane dirt track, runs 10 miles in a relatively straight line west to east from Number Four Road to Stillwater Reservoir or the intersection with Big Moose Road. Along the way, it takes you to a canoe put-in point on the north shore of Lake Francis and to two access roads—McCarthy Road and Basket Factory Road—as well as to the boat-launching site on the west shore of Stillwater Reservoir.

Both roads intersect a network of snowmobile trails; McCarthy Road takes you to small but attractive Sunday Lake, and Basket Factory Road allows you to reach Fifth Creek Pond.

Big Moose Road provides access to a foot trail leading to a manned fire tower on the top of Stillwater Mountain.

110   Lake Francis

Canoeing, fishing, swimming

With a hidden bog, pine-covered eskers along its northeastern shore, and handsome little rock islands, Lake Francis is certainly one of the most attractive lakes in the region. Although relatively large, a mile long and two-thirds of a mile wide, this body of water is shallow, providing only a warm-water fishery, limited to chain pickerel and yellow perch. In 1986 the state had plans for stocking the lake with tiger muskellunge.

With the exception of two private holdings on the north shore, the lake is entirely state-owned. An esker covered with tall white pine traverses the southeastern part of the lake, almost isolating a large area of marsh and bog accessible to canoeists. Smooth boulders ring parts of the southern shore, but as with most lakes in the north country, trees grow right to the lake edge, providing no exposed beach areas.

You will see herons and nesting loons as you paddle quietly along the shores. The lake's many bays and irregular shape extend its shoreline to allow for a nearly 4-mile paddle.

The lake's northern edge almost touches Stillwater Road, so access to the lake is easy. The canoe carry is no more than 20 yards. Stillwater Road widens at the access point to make off-road parking easy and safe.

On the northeast side of the lake a lane leads back a short distance to one of the private inholdings. The short section of this road on state land is beautifully canopied with stately pines in which ravens may be seen.

111 McCarthy Road to Sunday Lake and Wild Forest Boundary

Road, snowmobile trail, skiing, fishing
5.5 miles, 2½ hours, moderately hilly

From Lake Francis, it is 2.5 miles on Stillwater Road to the intersection with McCarthy Road; a state sign designates it as a snowmobile trail. This southbound, single-lane dirt road can double as a cross-country ski trail in winter. During the other seasons, it serves as a major hiking trail to some of the more remote places in the north-central area of the Wild Forest's northern region.

One of the immediate benefits of this road is the access it provides to a small but beautiful body of water, Sunday Lake. It is small enough to be more deserving of the name "pond," but its clear, blue water and enclosing circle of tall trees give it a special charm.

McCarthy Road ties into a snowmobile loop made up of Emmett Hill Road, the eastern portion of Panther Pond Loop, section 114, and North Crossover Trail. This loop is 7 miles long.

The northern portion of McCarthy Road can be driven by passenger car, although some rough spots will be encountered en route, mostly of the water-filled pothole variety. The road, running through thick forest over fairly level ground, makes a good hiking trail. However, if you wish to hike the southern half of the road or include the snowmobile loop, you can drive the first 3 miles to shorten your total hiking distance.

An added attraction of this hiking route is that it takes you to some remote streams—so remote that the DEC has not fully surveyed them to determine the extent of the fish population. It is known that such faraway streams as Hitchcock Creek, where McCarthy Road terminates, contain a population of naturally reproducing wild brook trout. No stocked fish are found here. This is true backcountry with a strong wilderness flavor.

About 0.5 mile south of Stillwater Road, McCarthy Road is intersected by Sunday Lake Road, a narrow route that takes you in 0.5 mile to the western edge of Sunday Lake. McCarthy Road is level, but Sunday Road pitches downward, and the descent becomes more noticeable as you near the lake. Like other routes in this section, the road runs through thick stands of hardwood that completely canopy the road.

You arrive at a small, open area on lake's edge with a makeshift fireplace and a site that can be used for tenting. With the exception of this spot, the lake has no exposed shoreline to allow hiking or exploring. Trees grow down to the water and aquatic vegetation extends from the shore into the lake.

Fishing is not easy here. Nonetheless, the lake contains sizeable populations of several species of fish—brook trout, yellow perch, sunfish, and bullheads.

State plans call for extending the trail northward along the lake's western boundary and then eastward to intersect Basket Factory Road. The extension would be a little over 0.5 mile and would be designated as a snowmobile route. It could also serve as a Nordic ski trail.

Back on McCarthy Road, you continue southward for 0.7 mile where you meet the McCarthy Crossover Trail, which has been closed as a snowmobile route by the state. The route is clearly visible but leads to wet areas near Sunday Creek. There are five small bog ponds immediately south of Sunday Lake that can be reached by bushwhacking northward for 0.5 mile from a point about 0.5 mile in on the old McCarthy Crossover Trail.

The terrain becomes more hilly as McCarthy Road continues south; low hills now can often be seen on both sides of the road, even though the road tends to stay on level land. From McCarthy Crossover Trail, it is a gradual climb for the next mile to bring you to the North Crossover Trail, a snowmobile trail intersecting from the west, which is barred to prevent automobiles from entering. If you have been driving, this is a good place to park; McCarthy Road is only suitable for four-wheel-drive vehicles south of this point.

Now McCarthy Road skirts the lower slopes of a small hill on the right and then descends into a low area with water on both sides of the road in wet seasons. In a mile you come to a fork. The right leg puts you on Emmett Hill Road, section 113, which would let you return to your vehicle via the Emmett Hill Road-Panther Pond Loop-North Crossover Trail. The left leg is the continuation of McCarthy Road, section 112.

112 McCarthy Road Trail to Hitchcock Creek

Hiking, skiing, fishing, snowmobiling
2.5 miles, 1½ hours, hilly

The continuation of McCarthy Road takes you in 2 miles to the road's end on the west side of Hitchcock Creek. Just before reaching the creek, McCarthy Road touches the Wild Forest boundary where a barrier prevents you from crossing into private property that is a part of the Webb Tract.

McCarthy Road snakes through terrain that has become increasingly more hilly. Immediately after leaving the intersection with Emmett Hill, you cross a small stream, Hay Creek. Crossing a few hillocks, McCarthy Road runs south and then turns northeast. In a little less than a mile, it passes a gravel pit on the left and then crosses a large stream, Fifth Creek, which has its headwaters in Fifth Creek Pond two miles to the north. As a fishing stream, it looks promising, but there is no data on its population.

After crossing Fifth Creek, you start uphill as the trail snakes back and forth; then you make a gradual descent to the Wild Forest boundary. The trail, however, turns at the barrier and swings north past a beaver meadow on the right. The trail now hugs the high ground overlooking Hitchcock Creek for 0.3 mile to the intersection with a closed snowmobile trail called the Basket Factory Trail. Here is a good place for a snack and some fishing for the creek contains wild brook trout.

113 Emmett Hill Road Trail

Road, snowmobile trail, fishing, hiking, cross-country skiing
1.7 miles, 1 hour, relatively level

Emmet Hill Road is a connecting link with the Number Four Road and trails near the Independence River. After leaving McCarthy Road, Emmett Hill Road stays on high ground as it heads in a southeasterly direction on the west side of Hay Creek. This is a route used by four-wheel-drive vehicles. The road stays well to the west of a large, open, swampy area in which beaver are active, bringing you in 1.7 miles to a junction on the northern bank of Fifth Creek near another wet area. The junction, incidentally, is on the county line separating Lewis County on the west from Herkimer County. The point is at the Wild Forest's boundary and all the land south and east is part of the privately owned Webb Tract. Here the trail meets the Panther Pond Loop Trail.

114 Panther Pond Loop and North Crossover Trail

Snowmobile trail
5.8 miles, 2½ hours, relatively level

Panther Pond Loop Trail connects the Number Four Road via Smith Road on the north with trails along the Independence River in the south. Emmett Hill Road meets Panther Pond Loop Trail at the junction described

Lower End of Panther Pond

in section 113. From the junction, the loop trail heads south for 1 mile to the short connecting link, East Bridge Trail, section 91, that leads to the river and to Balsam Flats.

The loop can also be used as an alternate return route for that section's hike. This is a deep forest trail with no noteworthy landmarks on this trail, just a mix of level stretches and small hillocks.

This upper portion of the Panther Pond eastern loop follows an old logging road. At 0.5 miles north, the road goes through a low, damp area and at 1.2 miles it passes to the north of a small pond, the headwaters of Third Creek, both too far south to be seen from the trail. At 3.5 miles you pass a gravel pit and the junction with two other trails—Lean-to Spur, heading southwest, and North Crossover Trail, heading east.

Turn onto North Crossover Trail. After a short, gradual rise, the trail moves onto flat land and continues on this tabletoplike terrain for 1.5 miles. At the 2-mile mark, it hugs the high ground a stone's throw from the south side of the headwaters of Pine Creek and then climbs gradually as it crosses a low hill to intersect McCarthy Road on the other side. Like the Panther Pond Loop section, this trail contains no noteworthy landmarks; it is primarily a deep forest trail running over level terrain.

115 Basket Factory Road to Fifth Creek Pond and Hitchcock Creek

Road, snowmobile trail, skiing, fishing
5.5 miles, 2¼ hours, hilly in the south

Drive 0.5 mile east of McCarthy Road along Stillwater Road to the intersection of Basket Factory Road, which runs southeast for 2.4 miles to a road barrier at Sunday Creek. While open to motorized vehicles, the single-lane dirt track is rough and you should exercise caution traveling it. Four-wheel-drive vehicles and ATVs can handle it easily. Beyond the creek, Basket Factory Trail continues south past Fifth Creek Pond, then south-southwest to Hitchcock Creek. The trail portion has been marked as a snowmobile trail in the past but it will no longer be maintained as such. It terminates at the end of McCarthy Road, section 111.

The origin of the road's name is a bit hazy. Local accounts hold that ash trees here were harvested in the late 1800s and transported to a factory in Lowville where wooden baskets were manufactured. While this is uncertain, the route itself has a number of attractive features.

If you choose to walk its length, the northern road section is an easy foot trail with varied terrain and vegetation. The trail connects with the East Loop Snowmobile Trail, section 116, which can be used to vary the route and create an ideal cross-country ski route. And, if you like fishing, both trails take you to various access points on Sunday Creek where wild and stocked brook trout are found. These are pretty good entrees for an outdoor menu, especially if you can take time to savor all the offerings.

Basket Factory Road crosses Sunday Creek 0.5 mile south from the trailhead. Actually the road crosses the creek at its confluence with Lizard Spring Brook, which flows from the east. This brook, too, holds brook trout. In another 0.5 mile, there is a bridge over a small tributary of Sunday Creek. This whole area, east and south of Sunday Lake, is a large wetland, covering a little more than a square mile, with a number of small ponds, some of which are bogs. The nearest bog is only 0.2 mile west of the road. Here, too, you find eskers. The area of low growth and swamps is home to colonies of beaver, who have impounded stretches of Sunday Creek. In winter, this whole area becomes one of the region's larger deer yarding places.

As you travel southeast, you will notice the land becoming hillier, though the low areas remain wet and soggy. Basket Factory Road winds its way around the base of low hills for a mile to reach the north side of Sunday Creek and the second access point to this attractive trout stream. Here, there is a road barrier to block vehicular access to the snowmobile trails that begin here.

Cross the creek and continue south. The trail takes you over rolling, but low-relief terrain through a dense forest of hardwood. In 0.2 mile you meet the abandoned McCarthy Crossover Trail coming in from the west. The trail heads downhill and 0.7 mile further you meet the southern leg of the East Loop Trail coming from the east. If you continue south onto the Basket Factory Trail, a 0.2-mile walk brings you to the east side of Fifth Creek Pond. The pond is surrounded by low-growth vegetation found in what has the appearance of a swampy moat, so the pond's eastern shore cannot be reached in any direct fashion. However, if you leave the trail and bushwhack a short distance westward staying on high ground, you can get a good view of this remote and isolated warm water pond.

From here southwest, the trail will no longer receive maintenance, though it can still be used to reach Hitchcock Creek and the McCarthy Road, section 112.

116 East Loop Snowmobile Trail
Snowmobile trail, skiing, fishing, hiking
3.5 miles, 2 hours, slightly hilly

If you plan a trek to Fifth Creek Pond, section 115, you can vary the route by using this loop. The northern portion of the loop will eventually be a major snowmobile artery with trailhead near Stillwater. The southern portion will not receive maintenance as a snowmobile trail in the future.

The loop begins where Basket Factory Road ends at Sunday Creek, section 115. East Loop Road parallels Sunday Creek heading northeast for 0.5 mile, then north for 0.4 mile, then east for another 0.5 mile. In the future a barrier will be erected here and a new foot trail will be constructed over private land 3 miles to the east to Stillwater Road.

The section of trail south of East Loop Road, called the East Loop Trail, makes a 2-mile loop back to Basket Factory Road. This is a hiking-only trail and the only serious wet spot you will encounter is where the trail crosses the headwaters of Sunday Creek, the creek's third access point. Once south of the creek, the trail starts rising as it enters the hilly area of the Wild Forest. The vertical rise in the next mile is 100 feet, high enough to make you aware you have left flat country.

When the trail rejoins the Basket Factory Trail, you can turn south for 0.2 mile to Fifth Creek Pond, section 115, or return north to complete the loop. Note that if you walk all of Basket Factory Road, this loop extends to 9.5 miles of hiking or skiing.

117 Stillwater Tower

Short trail, fire tower, scenic vistas
1.2 miles, 40 minutes, 564-foot vertical rise

Stillwater Road continues east from McCarthy Road for 4 miles to the hamlet of Stillwater on the western side of Stillwater Reservoir. Here you find several homes, a restaurant, headquarters of the local forest ranger, and a heavily used boat ramp, where hundreds of power boats are launched each summer by water-loving recreationists.

Stillwater Road forks 0.5 mile west of this community, and Big Moose Road heads south. From the fork it is 2 miles on Big Moose Road to the trailhead for Stillwater Mountain.

As mountains go, this one is on the small side with an elevation of only 2264 feet, but in a region characterized by flatlands and plains, a hill this tall is unusual. Its fire tower allows you to enjoy some grand vistas that can be seen from the mountain top, the highest spot in the region. This mountain is just a hint of the high country to the north and west and marks the boundary of the low Adirondack foothills.

The red-marked trail is straight and well maintained. The steady uphill climb leads to a huge, smooth, flat rock outcrop, and on this platform, the tower has been erected. During the summer, the fire tower is manned, and you can climb to its top. From it you can see Beaver Lake, Mosher Reservoir, and Stillwater Reservoir in the north, Twitchell Lake and Big Moose Lake to the southeast, and scores of streams and ponds to the southwest.

As you climb the trail to the fire tower, you cross an old logging road. The left leg takes you in about a mile back to Big Moose Road, while the right leg takes you in a curve westward to the Stillwater Spur Trail from Basket Factory Road, see section 116.

The trailhead of this old logging road is located 0.5 mile south on Big Moose Road where the DEC will construct a snowmobile trailhead and designate this road as an official snowmobile trail. This route will pass north of a small, unnamed pond draining into Stillwater Reservoir before crossing into the Independence River Wild Forest. Its entire 2.5-mile length will be through an easement over private land.

References and Other Resources

References

Beetle, David H. *West Canada Creek and Up Old Forge Way*, reprinted as one volume by North Country Books, Old Forge, New York 1972. *West Canada Creek*, originally published in 1946, and *Up Old Forge Way*, originally published in 1948 by the Utica *Observer-Dispatch*.

Dunham, Harvey L. *Adirondack French Louie – Early Life in the Woods*. Sylvan Beach, New York: North Country Books, 1978. Originally published privately by Harvey L. Dunham, Boonville, New York, 1953.

Grady, Joseph F. *The Adirondacks: Fulton Chain – Big Moose Region, The Story of a Wilderness*. Old Forge, New York: North Country Books, 1933. Second edition 1966.

O'Donnell, Thomas C. *Birth of a River: An Informal History of the Headwaters of the Black River*, Boonville, New York: Black River Books, 1952.

Simms, Jeptha R. *Trappers of New York*, Albany: J. Munsell, 1857. Reprinted by Harbor Hill Books, 1980.

Sperry, Charles B. and Claire C. *North Lake, The Jewel of the Adirondack*. Privately printed pamphlet, Whitesboro, New York, 1981.

Thomas, Howard. *Black River in the North Country*. Prospect, New York: Prospect Books, 1978.

Panorama from Stillwater Tower

3 G Fire Department. *History of Glenfield, Greig, and Brantingham.* Private-ly printed, no date.

Unit Management Plan for the Independence River Wild Forest. Albany: New York State Department of Environmental Conservation, 1986.

Other Resources

Adirondack Mountain Club, 174 Glen Street, Glens Falls, New York 12801

New York State Department of Environmental Conservation (DEC), 50 Wolf Road, Albany, New York 12233
Region 6 Headquarters, Washington Street, Watertown, New York 13601
Region 6, Canton Office, 30 Court Street, Canton, New York 13617
Region 6, Herkimer Office, 225 North Main Street, Herkimer, New York 13350
Region 6, Lowville Office, Lowville, New York 13367

For other things to do in the Adirondacks:
"I Love New York" series: *Camping, Tourism Map, State Travel Guide.* New York State Department of Commerce, Albany, New York 12245.
Adirondack Museum, Blue Mountain Lake, New York 12812

To find your way around the back roads:
Adirondack Region Atlas, City Street Directory, Poughkeepsie, New York. $3.75

Index

Guidebooks from Backcountry Publications

State Parks and Campgrounds
State Parks and Campgrounds in Northern New York, by John Scheib $9.95

Walks and Rambles Series
Walks and Rambles on the Delmarva Peninsula, by Jay Abercrombie $8.95
Walks and Rambles in Westchester (NY) and Fairfield (CT) Counties, by Katherine Anderson $7.95
Walks and Rambles in Rhode Island, by Ken Weber $8.95

Biking Series
25 Bicycle Tours in Maine, by Howard Stone $8.95
25 Bicycle Tours in Vermont, by John Freidin $7.95
25 Bicycle Tours in New Hampshire, by Tom and Susan Heavey $6.95
20 Bicycle Tours in the Finger Lakes, by Mark Roth and Sally Waters $7.95
20 Bicycle Tours in and around New York City, by Dan Carlinsky and David Heim $6.95
25 Bicycle Tours in Eastern Pennsylvania, by Dale Adams and Dale Speicher $7.95

Canoeing Series
Canoe Camping Vermont and New Hampshire Rivers, by Roioli Schweiker $6.95
Canoeing Central New York, by William P. Ehling $8.95
Canoeing Massachusetts, Rhode Island and Connecticut, by Ken Weber $7.95

Hiking Series
50 Hikes in the Adirondacks, by Barbara McMartin $9.95
50 Hikes in Central New York, by William P. Ehling $8.95
50 Hikes in the Hudson Valley, by Barbara McMartin and Peter Kick $9.95
50 Hikes in Central Pennsylvania, by Tom Thwaites $9.95
50 Hikes in Eastern Pennsylvania, by Carolyn Hoffman $9.95
50 Hikes in Western Pennsylvania, by Tom Thwaites $9.95
50 Hikes in Maine, by John Gibson $8.95
50 Hikes in the White Mountains, by Daniel Doan $9.95
50 More Hikes in New Hampshire, by Daniel Doan $9.95
50 Hikes in Vermont, 3rd edition, revised by the Green Mountain Club $8.95
50 Hikes in Massachusetts, by John Brady and Brian White $9.95
50 Hikes in Connecticut, by Gerry and Sue Hardy $8.95
50 Hikes in West Virginia, by Ann and Jim McGraw $9.95

The above titles are available at bookstores and at certain sporting goods stores or may be ordered directly from the publisher. For complete descriptions of these and other guides, write: Backcountry Publications, P.O. Box 175, Woodstock, VT 05091.

Lee M. Brenning is employed as an engineering technician at General Electric in Utica, New York and lives on his family's farm outside Barneveld, where he learned a reverence for the land at an early age. Independent study of local history and the environment led him to become deeply involved with New York State Forest Preserve issues. Advocates of low-impact recreation, Lee and his wife, Georgianna, are extensively exploring the Adirondacks in all seasons.

Lee's part in this guide took him on hiking, skiing, and snowshoeing trips throughout the Black River Wild Forest. His writing on this area reflects both a love of bushwhacking and an avid interest in local history.

Photo by Georgie Brenning

Photo by Barbara McMartin

A versatile outdoorsman, Bill Ehling is well equipped to describe hiking in this region. For years he has explored trails in central New York and the western Adirondacks — either on foot or on skis — and has helped to develop many of them. Past president of both the Finger Lakes Trail Conference and the Central New York Ski Touring Club, Bill is also active in the Onondaga Chapter of the Adirondack Mountain Club. He is a professor in the School of Public Communications at Syracuse University and is the author of 50 Hikes in Central New York.

Bill's contribution to this guide is the section covering the Independence River Wild Forest. His fascination with the glacial geology of the area and the development of the unusual sand plains region gives a special focus to the descriptions of the roads and trails.